BLOODY ENGLISH HISTORY

CAMBRIDGE

DAVID BARROWCLOUGH

The
History
Press

For Amie, in memory of her father and my brother, Adam
1970–2014

First published in 2015

The History Press
The Mill, Brimscombe Port
Stroud, Gloucestershire, GL5 2QG
www.thehistorypress.co.uk

© David Barrowclough, 2015

The right of David Barrowclough to be identified as the
Author of this work has been asserted in accordance with the
Copyright, Designs and Patents Act 1988.

All rights reserved. No part of this book may be reprinted
or reproduced or utilised in any form or by any electronic,
mechanical or other means, now known or hereafter invented,
including photocopying and recording, or in any information
storage or retrieval system, without the permission in writing
from the Publishers.
British Library Cataloguing in Publication Data.
A catalogue record for this book is available from the British Library.

ISBN 978 0 7509 6158 5

Typesetting and origination by The History Press
Printed in Great Britain

CONTENTS

ACKNOWLEDGEMENTS

T HE IDEA FOR THIS volume came out of my earlier book, *Ely: The Hidden History*, written with Kate Morrison Ayres, and partly relies on research and conversations we had together. Much of the knowledge for that book, and by extension this, began as an undergraduate student at Cambridge, where an interest in the history and archaeology of the local area was sparked by the lectures of Charles French and staff of both the Cambridge Archaeological Unit and Oxford Archaeology (East). Later I was to become co-editor of the *Proceedings of the Cambridge Antiquarian Society*, with my dear friend Dr Mary Chester-Kadwell, and something of what she taught me has no doubt rubbed off here; I hope it meets her high standards. This was a formative time for my understanding of the history of Cambridge, and much of what I absorbed reading my way into that role underpins the text presented here. The act of writing itself has always been my greatest consolation in difficult times, and producing this volume has been a great support at what turned out to be the most personally challenging time of my life. I thank my parents, family and friends for their support. Finally I thank Cate Ludlow at The History Press for encouraging me to write this book. I have attempted to check and double-check my sources, which are to be found in the bibliography at the end of the book, but for any errors or omissions that have slipped through I offer my apologies, mea culpa.

This book has only been possible thanks to the generous access granted to me by the following libraries, the librarians of which I would like to thank: The Lee Library, Wolfson College; The Cambridge Collection, housed in Cambridge Central Library; Cambridge University Library; The Haddon Library of Archaeology and Anthropology, University of Cambridge; Cambridge County Council Historic Environment Record.

ABOUT THE AUTHOR

David Barrowclough is a fellow of Wolfson College, University of Cambridge, where he is Tutor and Director of Studies. He has lived and worked in Cambridge for the last fifteen years, and has a particular interest in the history of the city. David has written and lectured widely on the history and archaeology of Cambridge, and is past editor of the *Proceedings of the Cambridge Antiquarian Society* as well as the author of *Ely: The Hidden History*, also published by The History Press.

AD 697

ETHELDREDA: BORN A PRINCESS, DIED A SAINT

ETHELDREDA'S BODY HAD lain buried for seventeen years when in *c.* AD 697 Wilfred and her physician Cynefrid witnessed her exhumation. What they saw astonished them. Her body was not only completely intact, with not a sign of decay, but the tumour on her neck, from which she had died, was completely healed. This was a miracle befitting a saint.

A Victorian view of Saint Etheldreda. (THP)

Etheldreda, also known as Audrey, was born into the East Anglian royal family. Her father was King Anna, whose seat was at Exning, but whose kingdom encompassed Cambridge. Married twice but always a virgin, she left her second husband to found a monastery at Ely in AD 673. With her small convent of nuns she restored an old church, reputedly destroyed by Penda, pagan king of the Mercians, and built her monastery on the site of what is now Ely Cathedral. After its restoration in AD 970 by Ethelwold it became the richest abbey in England, second only to Glastonbury, and around it the prosperous city of Ely, with its market and fair, grew.

In around AD 680 Etheldreda died from a tumour on the neck. This was reputedly a divine punishment for her vanity in wearing necklaces in her younger days. In reality it was the result of the plague, which also killed several of her nuns, who included amongst their number her sisters and nieces. In her memory at the annual St Audrey's Fair in Ely, held on 23 June, necklaces of silk and lace were sold. These were often of very inferior quality, hence the derivation of the word tawdry from St Audrey.

IRON AGE GIANTS

According to ancient tradition, the two giants, Magog and Gog, are buried in the hills south-east of Cambridge, and that a golden chariot was buried in a tumulus called Mutlow Hill.

Although such traditions are easy to dismiss as flights of fancy, in this case it is known that until the early eighteenth century there was, carved into the turf, the figure of a giant. Later in the eighteenth century all trace of the figures was lost when trees were planted over the site.

In the 1950s, archaeologist T.C. Lethbridge led an investigation of the site in an attempt to rediscover the carvings and shed light on the legend. Using a sounding bar he systematically tested the chalk hill and claimed to have rediscovered a carving of Epona, the Celtic horse goddess. He pronounced that the three-breasted goddess travelled across the side of Gog Magog with her beaked horse. To one side was a carving of a warrior equipped with a sword and shield, and to the other a curious figure wearing a cloak. He thought that the central figure had been made by the Iron Age tribe of the Iceni, famous for their leader Boudicca, who valiantly led the resistance against the Roman army. This central figure represented the Magog, or Mother Goddess, known to the Celts as Epona. The other two figures are slightly later in date, and were added by the incoming Catuvellauni tribe.

Standing 240ft (75m) high, the hill commands views of the region, and for this reason was chosen as the location for the construction of a fortress, built during the Iron Age. The oldest recorded activity is in 1574 when it was decreed by the university 'that no scholar of what degree soever he be, shall resort or go to any play or game either kept at Gog-Magog Hills or elsewhere within five miles of Cambridge'.

On finding that her exhumed body, and the linen shroud wrapped around her, were as fresh as the day of her funeral, she was declared a saint. A simple wooden coffin no longer sufficed for such a worthy person, and so the monks from her abbey procured a sarcophagus from the Roman cemetery on the edge of Cambridge at Grantchester. This was brought down the river to Ely where she was reburied with great ceremony; the fate of the original Roman occupier of the stone coffin is not recorded.

St Etheldreda's shrine was a site of pilgrimage until 1541, when it was cruelly destroyed. It had been thought that the story ended here, but in 1811 her hand was discovered, hidden away, near Arundel. Clearly, clergy had got wind of the impending iconoclasm, and took steps to preserve what they could of the saint. Her hand now resides in the Roman Catholic church of St Etheldreda, Ely, where presumably it will rest until a shrine befitting her importance is reconstructed in the cathedral.

AD 1010

VANQUISHED BY THE VIKINGS

IN **1010 IT IS** recorded that Cambridge was looted and completely burned to the ground by Viking raiders. This was particularly harsh as the town had, perhaps unwillingly, played host to the Danish army for a whole year in AD 870. The *Anglo-Saxon Chronicles* records that the Viking army led by kings Godrum, Oscytel and Anwynd also passed through Grantebrycge, the old name for Cambridge, in spring AD 874, after they had wintered at Repton. 'Passing through' sounds innocuous, but the reality was that each visit required

Vikings invading; the Danes sacked the city in 1010. (THP)

the townspeople to feed and supply the army – a significant burden, especially when they chose to stay a whole year.

The town's attraction lay partly in its strategic location, as a major crossing point across the River Cam (formerly known as the Granta). The *Anglo-Saxon Chronicles* tells us that the wooden bridge was built by King Offa (AD 756–793) when the town was known foremost as a port. Just a few years after the Vikings had passed through Cambridge they returned to settle. In some documents they are referred to as Irish merchants, which implies that they had come from Dublin, which was a major Viking port and settlement.

In AD 921 the townspeople swore allegiance to the English king, Edward the Elder, which subsequently helped earn it the right to mint coins and act as the local administrative centre. This tranquil scene was marred by a final Danish raid in 1010 when the town was looted and burnt. At this time if not all, then all but a few, buildings were constructed from wood,

On the river: the River Cam opposite King's, showing barges towed by horses.

which would easily have burned in a fire. The town was defended by a ditch and bank, topped with a wooden palisade. This would have offered some protection, but again, its wooden construction rendered it susceptible to the enemy's torch.

By the time of the Domesday Book in 1086, Cambridge probably had a population of about 2,000. By the standards of the time it was a medium-sized town. Later in the Middle Ages the population of Cambridge probably rose to about 3,000.

A coin of Edward the Elder; he gave Cambridge the right to run its own mint here. (THP)

FIRE, DEATH AND
MURDER AT THE FAIRS

'FIRE! FIRE!' RANG out the cry amongst the crowd. In a state of confusion, people started to push towards the exits. Performers called for calm from the stage, but another cry of 'Fire!' put paid to that. Managers standing in the auditorium tried to reassure the audience that there was

King John first granted the right to hold the three-day-long Stourbridge Fair in 1199 in order to raise money to support the patients of the Leper Hospital of St Mary Magdalene. (THP)

no fire, but they were in no mood to take any chances and continued to squeeze towards the narrow doors of the Stourbridge Fair Theatre. People in the upper boxes and gallery feared they would be trapped and began to attempt to climb down into the pit; some made it safely, whilst others fell on the way down, many were injured. As the weight of people pressing to get out increased, people began to panic, and three children, Esther Cook aged 12, Mary Freeman aged 13 and John Smith aged 14 were trampled to death along with Rose Mason, aged 24. To compound the tragedy, there never had been a fire. Instead, a gang of thieves had cried 'fire' in order to upset the audience, thus creating an opportunity for them to pickpocket in the confusion. Realising that their plan had gone badly awry, they slipped away amongst the crowd, and despite a reward of 100 guineas being posted on 29 September 1803, they were never identified.

Stourbridge Fair dates to 1199, when King John granted the Leper Hospital of St Mary Magdalene at 'Steresbrigge' in Cambridge a dispensation to hold a three-day fair in order to raise money to support the lepers. The fair was held between 12 and 14 September each year on the open land of Stourbridge Common beside the River Cam. Over the years it was gradually extended until it lasted three weeks.

Variously known as 'Stirbitch', 'Sturbritch' and latterly 'Stourbridge', the fair began with a proclamation. Alderman Newton records in his diary for 1668 that this was a convivial process. The aldermen and councillors gathered at the house of the alderman elected to be mayor for the forthcoming year. There they enjoyed sugar cakes, washed down with a glass of 'sack' (Spanish white wine). They then all rode to the fairground where the proc-lamation was read, before the party retired to the Guildhall. Again more sack and cakes were enjoyed, before everyone returned to the mayor-elect's house for a lavish dinner consisting of:

2 dishes of boyled chickens then a leg of mutton boyled, then a peece of rost beefe, then a mutton pasty, then a glass of Clarett round, then 2 couple of rebbetts, 2 couple of small wildfoule, and 2 dishes of tarts 3 in a dish.

Sixty years later the procession of aldermen and councillors had expanded so that in 1727 it consisted of, in order:

The Crier in Scarlet on horseback.
28 petty Constables on foot.
Three Drums.
Banners and Streamers.
The grand Marshal.
Two Trumpets.
The Town Music (12 in number).
Two French Horns.

The Bellman in state with the stand
    on Horseback.
Four Serjeants at Mace on Horseback.
The Mayor in his robes mounted on
    a Horse richly caparisoned, led by
    two footmen called redcoats with
    white wands.
The two representatives in Parliament
    on Horseback.
Twelve Aldermen according to
    seniority on Horseback (three
    and three) in their proper robes,
    the six seniors having their horses
    attended by as many Henchmen or
    redcoats with wands.
The Twenty four Common
    Councilmen three and three
    according to seniority.
Eight Dispencers in their Gowns
    (two and two).
Four Bailiffs in their habits
    (two and two).
The Gentlemen and Tradesmen of
    the Town.

Given this expansion it is not surprising that after 1758 the procession was curtailed, 'owing it is said to the trouble and charge of keeping it in a suitable condition'. However, it seems that the aldermen were happy to continue the age-old custom of feasting. Henry Gunning's description of the 1789 proc-lamation describes how, after mulled wine, sherry and cakes in the Senate House, 'the Vice-Chancellor, Bedells, Proctors, Taxors and the Commissary and others rode in carriages to the fair, where the Registrary read the proclamation, which was repeated by the Yeoman Bedell in three different places'. After this they retired to the 'Tiled Booth' (known later as the 'Oyster House'), passing through an upper room to the 'University Dining Room'. Here they were joined by numbers of Masters of Arts 'who had come for the express purpose of eating oysters. This was a very serious part of the day's proceedings and occupied a long time'. With barely a pause for breath this lavish lunch was followed shortly after by a lavish dinner:

The Tiled Booth, or Oyster House, in 1957.

> Before the Vice-Chancellor was placed a large dish of herrings; then followed in order a neck of pork roasted, an enormous plum pudding, a pease-pudding, a goose, a huge apple pie, and a round of beef in the centre. On the other half of the table the same dishes were placed in similar order (the herrings before the senior proctor) ...
>
> ... The Corporation proclaimed the fair, and had their dinner also; but it possessed this advantage over ours, that it was given at a private house where they were served with an abundance of venison and game.

Whilst the pillars of Cambridge society were enjoying themselves at the Tiled Booth, the townspeople and students were letting their hair down outside.

Caius College and Senate House in the early twentieth century. (LOC, LC-DIG-ppmsc-08079)

Esquire Bedell and Yeoman Bedwell.

Sixteenth-century records describe vulgar and indecent behaviour, perhaps described best by John Bunyan, who based *Vanity Fair* on his Cambridge experiences. Another famous visitor was Daniel Defoe, who visited in 1723. He regarded it the greatest fair in the world, with goods for sale from all parts of England and the Continent. Such was its renown that hackney coaches from London had brought visitors since at least 1605; as many as fifty made the journey in 1723.

With the throngs of people came fun, but also theft, with shoplifting not uncommon, as Edward Ward describes:

> Some that have no money come to buy books, whilst others, who want it, take 'em slily up, upon condition to pay if they're catch'd', hiding the books in a gown sleeve.

He describes the patter of a famous book auctioneer:

> Here's an old author for you, gentlemen, you may judge his antiquity by the fashion of his leather-jacket; herein is contained, for the benefit of you scholars, the knowledge of everything ... For your encouragement, gentlemen, I'll put him up at two shillings ... What? Nobody bid? ... Fye, for shame, why sure men of your parts and learning will never suffer the works of so famous an author to be thus under-valued ... What? Nobody amongst you gentlemen of the black robe, that has so much respect for the wisdom of our ancestors, as to advance t'other threepence?

Proctors patrolled the fair on the lookout for 'naughty and corrupt behaviour', which often resulted from direct conflict between Town and Gown. For example, in 1701 the mayor and Corporation gave a company permission to perform plays at the fair, but the university swore in sixty-two

proctors who demolished the booth and imprisoned the celebrated actor Doggett, founder of the Thames Watermen's Badge. Similarly, in 1730, the Vice-Chancellor issued an edict stating:

> Whereas certain Players propose to Act Plays in an House erected near Paper Mills, and the Senate of the University have out of a just Resentment Discountenanced such Illegal Practices: I do hereby strictly charge and command all Scholars not to go There ... I do likewise forbid all under the Degree of Masters of Arts from going to Sturbridge Fair, without Consent of the Master or President of their particular College signified under his Hand Writing.

While the university had its proctors patrolling the fair, the mayor had eight sergeants, known as Red Coats, from their distinctive uniform. A call of 'Red Coat! Red Coat!' immediately brought one of these officials to the scene should there be any trouble, while the sergeants themselves kept a close eye out for cheats and pickpockets. Their constant cry of 'Look about you, there!' added to the bustle, noise and excitement of the fair. Disputes between merchants and purchasers, meanwhile, were settled by the mayor at the Court of Piepowders. One of the best-sounding jobs belonged to the Lord of the Taps, appointed to taste the ale sold in the various booths, to ensure it was in good condition. Records show that in 1655 the Corporation of Cambridge ordered that '... XXs. shall be given out of the moneys in the chest to Michael Wolfe towards the buyinge of a Coate

MURDER AT MIDSUMMER FAIR

The earliest Midsummer Fair was granted by King John c.1211 to the Priors and Canons of Barnwell.

For some, the coming together of so many people with ready cash proved too tempting an opportunity to ignore. In 1842, for example, William Haslop left Midsummer Fair for a romantic stroll with his girlfriend. The evening was warm and all seemed perfect as the pair walked along the banks of the River Cam. A group of three men walked past, then this gang doubled back, attacked Haslop, who fell to the ground, and piled on top of him. With one smothering his mouth and eyes,

Barnwell Priory in the 1900s: the Cellarer's Chequer. (F.G. Binnie)

another picked his pockets, taking 7 shillings. Whilst William was pinned to the ground his girlfriend made her escape, raising the alarm by shouting out, 'Murder! Murder!' The gang split up, two got clean away, but a third, leaping a hedge, found himself trapped in a dead end where he was arrested by a constable. This William Freeman was charged with assault and robbery on the Queen's Highway on 25 June 1842. At the Cambridge Assizes he denied any involvement, but was unconvincing, and convicted. The sentence: six months' hard labour.

against Sturbridge Fayer now next ensuinge, he being Lord of the Taps this present yeare.'

This coat was a distinctive feature of the office, being of crimson cloth decorated with barrel taps, described by Edward Ward in 1700 as 'like a porcupine with his quills, or looking rather like a fowl wrapped up in a pound of sausages'. He must have cut quite a figure as he walked about the fair as, according to John Bowtell, he was always 'preceded by a merry piece of music'.

As the fair grew in popularity, with coaches bringing visitors from all over the east of England as well as from London, there was a need for a greater presence to combat pickpockets and shoplifters. In the eighteenth century,

the larger-than-life character of Jacob Butler was put in charge of the fair:

In stature he was six feet four inches high, of determined character, and deemed a great eccentric because, among other reasons, he usually invited the giants and dwarfs, who came for exhibition, to dine with him. He was so rigid in seeing the charter literally complied with, that if the ground was not cleared by one o'clock on the day appointed, and he found any of the booths standing, he had them pulled down, and the materials taken away. On one occasion when the wares were not removed by the time mentioned in the charter, he drove his carriage among the crockery and destroyed a great quantity.

AD 1234

JOUSTING TOURNAMENTS

TOURNAMENTS WERE HELD regularly in Cambridge, to the amusement of the students and townspeople. The jousts were accompanied by drinking, card playing and gambling, much to the displeasure of the university authorities, who complained in around 1634, that:

> ... Much lewd people waited on these assemblies, light housewives as well as light horsemen repaired thereunto. Yea, such the clashing of swords, the rattling of arms, the neighing of horses, the shouting of men all day-time, with the roaring of riotous revelers all the night, that the Scholars' studies were disturbed, safely endangered ... charges enlarged, all provisions being unconsciously enhanced.

Just how 'commonly kept in Cambridge' were tournaments is shown by the records of King Henry III, who 'in the interests of the common peace' issued letters patent prohibiting earls, barons, knights and others from attending the tournaments arranged to be held in Cambridge in 1234, 1236 and 1246.

Clearly these orders were repeatedly ignored, otherwise there would have been no need to continually issue the prohibition. Certainly in 1245 the order was ignored by Sir Ralph de Kamoys, who was found guilty of keeping 'a riotous tilting on the border of the town'. For this offence the punishment was severe: his lands were seized by the king. They were, however, restored to him later, when he submitted to the Earls of Cornwall, Norfolk and Leicester. Henry III issued letters patent again in 1270. They forbid tournaments, tiltings, joustings or any other warlike games to be held in Cambridge, or within five miles of the town. The same ban was later imposed by Edward I and Edward II.

Despite these attempts, the popularity of tournaments meant that the authorities were fighting a losing battle in their proclamations to stop them. By tradition, tournaments were held on Mondays and Tuesdays. Two camps would be designated where the knights would lodge, with the actual tournament taking place on a field outside the principal settlement, where stands were erected for spectators. Parties were hosted in each settlement by the most senior nobles, and preliminary jousts called the 'vespers', or *premières commençailles*, offered knights a showcase for their talents.

On the day of the tournament the sides were formed of those 'within' the principal settlement, and those from the one 'outside'. Each side then paraded, calling out war cries, before the newest and youngest knights jousted with each other in front of the more senior knights and spectators. Then at mid-morning the knights lined up for the 'estor' or charge. At a signal from a herald the lines of knights rode at each other with levelled lances, the aim being to strike the opponent and unseat him from his

Edward I, who banned 'warlike' games in Cambridge. (THP)

horse. Those remaining on horseback after the first charge would then turn quickly and single out knights to attack. It is this act of turning from which the tournament takes its name. These encounters were demanding, and it was not unusual for the lance to break, in which case the knight could ride to the 'lists', a staked and embanked line in front of the stands, where squires stood with three replacement lances.

As the tournament continued, the mêlée would tend to degenerate into running battles between the two sides spread over several square miles. Knights sought to capture their opponents in order to hold them to ransom, with the fight continuing until both sides were exhausted, or evening came. At the end of the day lavish banquets and entertainments took place in the settlements, with prizes awarded to the best knight on either side.

There is no doubting the massive popularity of the tournament amongst the aristocracy; however, both royal and ecclesiastical authorities were less enthusiastic, and often used their power to prohibit these events. The usual ecclesiastical justification for prohibiting them was that it distracted the aristocracy from more acceptable warfare in defence of Christianity. In 1130 Pope Innocent II denounced the tournament and forbade Christian burial for those killed in them. However, the reason for the ban imposed on them in England by Henry II and his successors lay in its persistent threat to public order, with knights going to tournaments often accused of theft and violence against the public. Tournaments were allowed in England after 1192, when

Richard I identified six sites for them, provided patrons paid for a license, but both King John and his son, Henry III, introduced prohibitions as we have seen. These bans, such as the ones imposed in Cambridge, annoyed the aristocracy.

Jousting formed part of the tournament event as an evening prelude to the big day, and as a preliminary to the grand charge. It quickly developed its own devoted constituency, and in the 1220s began to hold its own exclusive events outside the tournament. The biographer of William 'John the Bastard' Marshal, observed in in about 1224 that in his day noblemen were more interested in jousting than tourneying, and about this time we have the first mention of an exclusively jousting

Jousting in its deadliest form – on a battlefield. (THP)

Edward III, who encouraged jousting in England. (THP)

event, the 'Round Table' held in Cyprus by John d'Ibelin, lord of Beirut. Round Tables were a thirteenth-century elimination jousting event held for knights and squires alike. By the fourteenth century the joust replaced the tournament, encouraged by King Edward III (1327–1377). In the last true tournament held in England in 1342 at Dunstable, the mêlée was postponed so long by jousting that the sun was sinking by the time the lines charged.

The term joust means 'a meeting' and came to refer to combat with a lance. During the fourteenth century a cloth barrier known as a tilt, from the Middle English 'a cloth covering', was introduced to separate the contestants, and 'tilt' came to be used as a term for the joust itself. The purpose of the tilt barrier was to prevent collisions and enable the knights to better

17

Sixteenth-century depiction of a tournament by Paulus Hector Mair; perfecting his treatise on martial arts became an obsession, and he eventually bankrupted his substantial estate to produce the collection this plate appeared in. He later took to embezzling funds from the Treasury, and was hanged as a thief in 1579. He was 62.

control their horses and concentrate on aiming the lance. Dedicated tiltyards with wooden barriers were built in England – Horse Guards Parade in London, for example, was formerly the tiltyard constructed by Henry VIII as an entertainment venue adjacent to Whitehall Palace. It was a permanent structure and apparently had room for 10–12,000 spectators, accommodated in conditions which ranged from the spartan to the opulent. The Accession Day tilts were held here in the reigns of Elizabeth I and James I. These were a highlight of the social calendar, as Elizabeth I found 'the whole chivalric nature of the tournament with its mock combat and heroic connotations ... peculiarly appealing'. The aristocrats who attended wore elaborate costumes 'designed and made for themselves and their servants'.

AD 1345

THE
BLACK DEATH

It is said that the plague takes three forms. In the first people suffer an infection of the lungs, which leads to breathing difficulties. Whoever has this corruption or contamination to any extent cannot escape but will die within two days. Another form ... in which boils erupt under the armpits ... a third form in which people of both sexes are attacked in the groin.

The Black Death arrived in England in 1345, bringing with it misery and death on an unprecedented scale. In Cambridge almost everyone who lived in the area near to the castle died, with those that survived quickly moving away while they could. Boccaccio's description is graphic:

In men and women alike it first betrayed itself by the emergence of certain tumours in the groin or armpits, some of which grew as large as a common apple, others as an egg ... From the two said parts of the body this deadly gavocciolo (buboe) soon began to propagate and spread itself in all directions indifferently; after which the form of the malady began to change, black spots or livid making their appearance in many cases on the arm or the thigh or elsewhere, now few and large, now minute and numerous. As the gavocciolo had been and still was an infallible token of approaching death, such also were these spots on whomsoever they showed themselves.

This was followed by acute fever and vomiting of blood, and then death. Most victims died two to seven days after first being infected.

After this first outbreak, the town was plagued by the Black Death continually through the fourteenth century, with major attacks in 1349, 1361 and 1369. Known to medieval people of the fourteenth century as either the 'Great Pestilence' or the 'Great Plague', the Latin name *atra mors* (Black Death) first appeared in 1631 in a book by J.I. Pontanus, who wrote about the plague of 1348, as *Vulgo & ab effectu atram mortem vocatibant* (Commonly and from [its] effects, they called [it] the black death).

Scientific knowledge had stagnated during the Middle Ages and so there

Contemporary scene from one of the era's many 'Dance of Death' collections, inspired by the ravages of the plague.

was little understanding of what had caused the plague. The most authoritative account at the time came from a report to the King of France that blamed the heavens, in the form of a conjunction of three planets in 1345 that caused a 'great pestilence in the air'. The idea that the plague was caused by bad air became the most widely accepted theory for the Black Death. In Cambridge in 1393 it was said that the 'Foul Lane', a route crossing what is now the Great Court of Trinity College, stank so abominably that many scholars fell sick because it. Thus, although the importance of hygiene was not scientifically established until the nineteenth century, it was already known anecdotally in Cambridge, and elsewhere, that the onset and spread of the Black Death could be prevented through the provision of a supply of fresh clean water, which allowed people to employ what we would consider essential hygiene.

Nonetheless it was still common for the streets to be filthy, populated with live animals of all sorts, and human faecal waste. In such conditions a transmissible disease will spread easily. Figures from Church records show that of 638 clergy in the diocese of Ely (of which Cambridge is part), at least 350 died of the plague. Overall the effect of the plague was to depopulate and impoverish the town. For some, however, it created new opportunities, for example to fill some of the vacant posts: Bishop Bateman founded the College of the Scholars of the Holy Trinity of Norwich, or Trinity Hall as we now know it, in a hostel previously used by monks from Ely.

Plague returned again towards the end of the sixteenth century, and attention again focused on hygiene. The King's Ditch, which partly enclosed the old town, was basically an open sewer, and was held responsible for the Great Plague in the town. The authorities, concerned about its filthy state, settled on the need for a supply of fresh clean water. Matthew Parker suggested in 1574 that 'the river at Wandlebury might be brought to the City of Cambridge to wash the King's Ditch'. His proposal was ambitious, requiring major engineering work, but nonetheless in 1610 the scheme was carried out. From Wandlebury an artificial channel was dug to the corner of Lensfield Road, where water was distributed down Trumpington Street and on to Market Hill. This work proved so successful that for the next 250 years it provided drinking water for the town. The ornate 'Hobson's Conduit', named after one of the men involved in planning and executing the works, was originally built in the market place, but was later removed to the corner of Lensfield Road, where it can still be seen.

AD 1381

PEASANTS' REVOLT

CAMBRIDGE WAS NOT immune from the anger that led to the Peasants' Revolt in 1381. Rioters focused their attention on the houses of William Wigmore, the Esquire Bedell, an unpopular local landowner. Having destroyed his property, the mob then turned its attention to Corpus Christi College, which they raided, burning its books and charters, before broadening their vengeance and sacking any house belonging to the university and burgesses.

It might be thought odd that Corpus should be the subject of so much anger as – alone amongst the Cambridge colleges – it owed its very existence to the townsmen who had founded it. The problem was that since its foundation it had become unjustly rich

Corpus Christi, raided by rioting peasants. (LOC, LC-DIG-ppmsc-08081)

through the implementation of an unfair 'candle rent' that it demanded from more than half the households in the town. This tax had originally been intended to be used to pay for candles to light guild services, but over the years it had been corrupted, allowing the college to amass a large surplus that it used for the purposes of the college. This included the purchase of much property within the town, making it one of the largest landlords in Cambridge.

The college's wealth and privileges were on conspicuous display each year during the Corpus Christi procession. Headed by the aldermen of the guild, followed by men carrying enamelled silver shields with coats of arms and symbols of the Passion, in order of procession, next came the master of the college. His grandeur was such that he was shielded from the elements by an ornate canopy, whilst he carried the Host in a richly decorated solid silver-gilt tabernacle. Behind him came in order: the vice-chancellor, the fellows and scholars of Corpus Christi, members of the university, the mayor, the Town Council, burgesses and many ordinary citizens, all of whom would be carrying torches. The procession went from the college first to the Great Bridge and then to all other parts of the town. Intended to impress, the ostentatious display of wealth and power also caused much resentment amongst the townspeople struggling to pay the harsh candle tax.

Corpus Christi may have taken the brunt of the town's anger but it was not the only college to be attacked. In the century preceding the Peasants' Revolt,

a total of eight colleges had been established in Cambridge. Together they owned much property in the town, giving the university ever-increasing levels of control over the townspeople's daily lives. On the second day of rioting this resentment came to a head when a mob seized jewels and vessels from Great St Mary's, broke open the University Chest, and burnt its charters and deeds in the Market Square.

Matters took a more structured form when the mayor and bailiffs intervened, not to stop the rioting, but instead to force the university and college authorities to sign deeds renouncing all their royal privileges. This unexpected turn of events illustrates just how distanced Town and Gown had become from each other during this period of university expansion. The riots continued into a third day: this time a mob of 1,000 men marched on Barnwell Priory, where they broke down walls enclosing former common land. The riots continued unabated until the Bishop of Norwich entered Cambridge with a body of armed men who quickly suppressed the revolt.

The mayor and his bailiffs were summoned to Westminster, where the deeds which the university authorities had been forced to sign were cancelled, and as punishment the king increased the taxes on the town and removed its franchises. Although these were restored a year later, it was now quite clear that if one of the aims of the revolt had been to force the university to conform to the laws and customs of the borough, it had failed. Instead the university was given increased jurisdiction over daily life within the borough, including such essential activities as the buying and selling of food and drink within Cambridge. Relations between the town and the university continued to be uneasy, and often hostile, for generations. Fuller, for example, gives the following account of relations between the university and the town in 1384:

First. That hereafter the oversight of all victuals should belong to the Chancellor; so that no townsman ever since putteth a crumb of bread or a drop of beer into his mouth, but what first is weighed and measured by an officer of the University.

Secondly. That the Chancellor and the university should have power to set prices on candles (very necessary, I assure you, to hard students) and to license all victualing-houses, and oversee all wares and weights at Stourbridge Fair.

Thirdly. That no action be brought by any townsman against Scholar or Scholar's servant save only in the Court of the Chancellor.

Fourthly. That the university have power to punish and amerce all fore-stallers, regrators etc paying a rent of ten pounds a year for that privilege into the Exchequer; this their power extending to the town and suburbs therof. We must not forget that all kinds of fuel, wood, coals, turf etc were then subjected to the Chancellor, as to set the price thereof.

Illustration from Froissart's Chronicles *showing the moment that the leader of the abortive rebellion, Wat Tyler, met his doom – decapitated by the Mayor of London. The Cambridge rebels used this outbreak as an opportunity to burn and sack properties in the city.*

AD 1553

BLOODY MARY'S REVENGE ON CAMBRIDGE

Edward VI, whose death began a terrible era for Cambridge. (THP)

KING EDWARD VI, THE surviving son of Henry VIII, died on 6 July 1553 at the age of only 15 years, throwing England into political turmoil. He had been ill since February, allowing time for him and his Council to draw up the 'Devise for the Succession', an attempt to prevent the country returning to Roman Catholicism. By this document he excluded his two half-sisters from the inheritance of the Crown, and instead named his Protestant cousin, Lady Jane Grey, as his heir and successor. Thus, upon news of Edward's death, the Council immediately proclaimed Lady Jane Grey queen.

The Council knew that Lady Mary (1516–1558), the oldest surviving child of Henry VIII, was unlikely to accept this state of affairs, and shortly after news of Edward's death had been made public the Privy Council received a message from Mary asserting her 'right and title' to the throne, and commanding that they proclaim her queen. The Council's reply was terse and to the point, stating that Jane was now queen by authority of Edward VI, whilst Mary was illegitimate and supported by only 'a few lewd, base people'. Nonetheless, the Duke of Northumberland knew that Mary was a threat to Jane's authority and so set off to arrest her. At the time Mary was at Sawston Hall, Cambridge.

The duke set off with an army of 8,000 men on foot and a further 2,000 on horseback, suggesting that he was anticipating that Mary would put up quite a fight. Certainly news had reached London that a number of nobles and gentlemen had rallied to her side, along with 'innumerable companies of the common people'. Many of those who rallied to her side were conservatives hoping for the defeat of Protestantism, but her supporters also included many for whom her lawful claim to the throne overrode religious considerations.

Leaving London on 14 July the duke's attempt to arrest Mary was already doomed to failure. He reached Cambridge the following day, only to hear that Mary had already recruited a force of 20,000 men. At this news Northumberland's army deserted, and worse still he heard that in his absence Mary had been proclaimed queen in London. The reign of Lady Jane Grey had lasted just nine days.

Northumberland found himself in a dire situation, and in a last-ditch attempt to save his skin, attempted to establish credentials as a supporter of Mary by proclaiming her queen in front of Cambridge market cross. His declaration was too little, too late, and he was arrested in King's College by the Earl of Arundel. He was carried off to London where, even though he renounced Protestantism, was executed by beheading on 22 August, followed shortly afterwards by Lady Jane Grey herself.

The title page of Cranmer's edition of the Bible. (THP)

The ruthless entrenchment of her position, together with her vicious suppression of Protestantism, deservedly earned Queen Mary the epithet 'Bloody'. She quickly reversed Edward's Protestant reforms and reunited the Church with Rome. Mass was once again celebrated in England. In Cambridge she directed a clampdown on the university. All of the masters of the colleges, except three, and many fellows were removed from their posts. At St John's College, fourteen fellows went into exile. From now on only those that subscribed to the Roman Catholic religion would be allowed to obtain a Cambridge degree. In 1556 Archbishop Parker instructed that surplices must be worn in church. Leading Protestants objected, and at St John's most of the members attended without surplices. The master was forced to promise that he would ensure that the instruction was obeyed. The Protestant bishops Latimer, Ridley and Cranmer, who had all been educated in Cambridge, now found themselves severely out of favour and were burned alive at Oxford, whilst John Hullier suffered a similar fate on Jesus Green, in Cambridge.

St John's chapel, as seen from the river, where Protestants protested by attending without wearing surplices. (LC-DIG-ppmsc-08088)

Mary's revenge was still incomplete, and a Commission was appointed to inspect the university and ensure that Roman Catholicism had been completely re-established. The members arrived in Cambridge in January 1557. They immediately forbade the celebration of Mass in Great St Mary's and St Michael's, because the eminent German Protestants, Martin Bucer and Paul Fagius, had been buried in these churches. They commanded in the name of the queen the exhumation of the corpses. The coffins were dragged from the churches, and bound to a stake on Market Hill. There they were burned, together with all the heretical books that the Commission had been able to discover in the colleges. On the following day, the Bishop of Chester undertook to cleanse Great St Mary's, beginning with a large tub of water, to which he added salt, ashes and wine. He then walked three times outside and three times inside Great St Mary's to purify the building. On the next day, there was a great procession, and St Michael's was similarly cleansed. Thus did Bloody Mary rightly earn her sobriquet and re-establish Roman Catholicism in the university.

The Buck brothers' depiction of Cambridge Castle in 1730.

AD 1556

BURNT AT THE STAKE: JOHN HULLIER, THE PROTESTANT MARTYR

JOHN HULLIER HAS the dubious distinction of being the only Protestant martyr to be burnt at the stake in Cambridge. He was educated at Eton College, before arriving at King's College, Cambridge, where he continued his education and became a fellow. In all likelihood Hullier had adopted Protestantism whilst a student, as although the books of Martin Luther were burnt in 1520, a number of Cambridge students were sympathetic with his doctrines. They had come to be known locally as 'the Germans', and met at the White Horse Inn, nicknamed 'Germany', which stood between the Bull and King's College. Prominent among these men were Robert Barnes, prior of the Austin Friars, and Hugh Latimer, a fellow of Clare. Barnes controversially preached a sermon in St Edward's in 1525, which criticised the pomp of the bishops and the church courts. For this he was accused of heresy, arrested and taken to London. There he was tried at Westminster before Cardinal Wolsey, and recanted. Although this probably saved his life, he was not allowed to return to Cambridge. Others accused,

and examined, by Wolsey included Latimer and other Cambridge men.

Thus by the time Hullier arrived at King's Cambridge had a well-established Protestant tradition. Among the Protestants teaching in Cambridge during Hullier's time were several prominent European scholars, one of whom, Martin Bucer, was from Strasbourg and whose teaching in Cambridge between 1549 and his death in 1551 influenced many leading men, most likely including Hullier. When Bucer died his funeral was attended by 3,000 people.

After his studies Hullier remained in Cambridgeshire, becoming a curate at the church in Brabraham and then moving to King's Lynn. During this time he preached Protestantism to the people of the Fens, who it is said avoided capture by using a pole to jump the dykes, and hiding in the plentiful reed beds. Alas, Hullier was less fortunate and early in the reign of Queen Mary, he was arrested. He was most likely first imprisoned in Ely before being transferred to Cambridge Castle, where he was held for a long time. During this period he wrote letters and prayers to his followers. In 1556 he was brought to trial in Cambridge and condemned to be burnt at the stake on Jesus Green, the only Protestant martyr to die in the town. The punishment was executed on Maundy Thursday, 2 April 1556. The Catholics present tried to scare off a number of Protestants who stood vigil to offer him their support, but they refused to leave. Hullier stood firm throughout the ordeal; picking up one of the Protestant texts that was burnt with him, a communion book, he read it whilst he burnt. As he finally succumbed to the flames he cried out, 'Lord Jesus, receive my spirit'.

BEAR-BAITING

BEAR-BAITING WAS ONE of the most popular pastimes of the sixteenth and seventeenth centuries, frequently leading to conflict between the university authorities and townspeople. The authorities complained that the organisers 'endevored by theire bearbaytinge and bullbaytings, and such like vaine games, to hinder the quiet of the Universitie, and to draw over the students from their books'.

As a result, the university implemented a ban on bear-baiting within five miles of Cambridge. However, this proved hard to enforce and the regulation was frequently ignored. In 1581 a bear was baited in Chesterton, well within the prescribed area, attracting the presence of a large number of students. The university proctor was sent to investigate:

> He there found the beare at stake, where he had been bayted in the sermon time, between one and two o'clock in the afternoon. He asked the bearward by what authoritie he bayted his beare there, who answered that he was Lord Vaux's man and had a warrant from the justices.

This warrant, the proctor said, was invalid as the university had jurisdiction, and he ordered the man to accompany them forthwith to the vice-chancellor. The people of Chesterton were not, however, going to be deprived of their sport and a fierce argument ensued. The crowd got hold of one of the proctors, and 'violently shoved and thrust the Bedell upon the beare, in sort that he cold hardly keepe himself from hurt'.

The parish constable and his brother also joined in defence of the bear-ward, the brother going so far as to say that 'if Evensong were done when the scholars had gone they would bayte in despight of them'.

The university ultimately came out top in this dispute and the constable was dismissed from his office by the vice-chancellor.

The difficulty the university had in prohibiting bear-baiting in Cambridge was in part due to the royal patronage that it enjoyed. In the sixteenth century one of its biggest enthusiasts was King Henry VIII whose support extended so far as to have a bear-pit constructed at his palace at Whitehall in London. Such 'bear-gardens' usually took the form of a circular fenced area, the 'pit', with seating for spectators around the outside. Within the pit, towards one edge, a post was planted, and the bear chained to it, either by the leg or neck. Into the pit were then released several Old English bulldogs selected and trained to fight the bear. During the course of the spectacle the dogs would be replaced by fresh animals as they tired, or were killed by the angry bear. In 1575 Robert Dudley, Earl of Leicester, put on a contest for Queen Elizabeth I at Kenilworth Castle. The spectacle was vividly described in a letter by Robert Laneham:

Henry VIII, an ardent fan of the bear-pit. (THP)

Thursday, the fourteenth of July, and the sixth day of her Majesty's coming, a great sort of bandogs [mastiff] were then tied in the outer court and thirteen bears in the inner ...

Well, the bears were brought forth into the court, the dogs set to them, to argue the points even face to face. They had learned counsel also on both parts, what may they be counted partial that are retained but to one side? I know not. Very fierce, both one and the other, and eager in argument. If the dog in pleading would pluck the bear by the throat, the bear with traverse would claw him again by the scalp, confess and a list, but avoid it could not that was bound to the bar, and his counsel told him that it could be to him no policy in pleading.

Therefore, with fending & proving, with plucking and tugging, scratching and biting, by plain tooth and nail on one side and the other, such expense of blood and leather [skin] was there between them, as a months licking (I think) will not recover, and yet remain as far out as ever they were.

It was a sport very pleasant, of these beasts, to see the bear with his pink eyes leering after his enemies approach, the nimbleness and wayt [wait] of the dog to take his advantage, and the force and experience of the bear again to avoid the assaults. If he were bitten in one place, how he would pinch in another to get free, that if he were taken once, then what shift, with biting, with clawing, with roaring, tossing and tumbling, he would work to wind himself free from them. And when he was loose, to shake his ears twice or thrice with the blood and the slather about his physiognomy, was a matter of goodly relief.

Bear-baiting in the Georgian era. As the advert promised, 'the Great Muscovy Bear' was to be 'baited at the Wrestler-Inn in the petty Cury, Cambridge'.

The queen was particularly keen on the fights, and when an attempt was made by a group of Puritans in 1583 to ban bear-baiting on Sundays, she personally intervened to overrule them, and it was not until 1835 that bear-baiting was banned by the Cruelty to Animals Act 1835.

In Cambridge bears continued to be baited as late as the eighteenth century. The following advertisement appeared in the *Cambridge Chronicle* of 30 November 1749:

This to acquaint the Publick that on Monday next in the Afternoon, the Great Muscovy Bear will be baited at the Wrestler-Inn in the petty Cury, Cambridge.

P.S. The said Bear will exhibit many extraordinary Performances Dec. 2, 1749.

The whole entertainment will conclude with a scene worthy Observations of the curious.

WITCHES AND WITCHCRAFT

SIXTEENTH-CENTURY **CAMBRIDGE WAS** awash with gossip and rumour about witches, and Witchcraft Acts were passed in 1563 and 1604. In 1579 'Two were hanged in Cambridge, mother and daughter, the mother said the devil had been true to her for three score years and she would not renounce him; the daughter died penitent'.

The hanging of witches, showing crowds of named 'familiars' under the gallows. Outbreaks of witch fever were frequent in this era, leading many to their deaths. This woodcut shows the deaths of so-called 'witches' at Chelmsford, Essex, in 1589.

Anyone arrested for witchcraft in Cambridge would be taken to the 'witches gaole', which in reality was part of the ordinary Cambridge prison within which a section was partitioned to separate witches from common criminals, with a third part occupied by debtors. Accounts for 1620 include an item, 'For amendinge the particion between the Witches gaole & the other felons gaole, xviijs', and then again in 1623, for 'a locke for the dore of ye witches gaiole' which cost 2s 4d. Conditions in the gaol, which occupied the gatehouse of the former castle, can only be described as appalling. Food was rationed to the extent that on market days the town crier collected scraps of food for the inmates.

What is striking is that the accounts should regularly specifically refer to an identifiable witches' gaol, suggesting that there was regular call upon these quarters. This is confirmed from the court records. In 1589, Cambridge physician Dr Barrow and William Butler of Clare Hall College were asked by Robert Throckmorton to diagnose his daughter's illness. Barrow examined Jane and pronounced that her fits were caused by witchcraft. In so doing he set in train a series of events that would eventually lead to her conviction and execution. A further case is recorded in 1645 when 'a woman was hanged at Cambridge for keeping a tame frog and it was sworn to be her imp'. Her name is not recorded, but elsewhere Botwell identifies 'the wife of one Lendale was hanged on Jesus Green for witchcraft', and John Stearne, in his *Discovery of Witchcraft* (1648), described 'one Lendall of Cambridge' who 'carried herself at her execution like a saint'.

To their eternal shame and damnation, ignorance and superstition were given academic authority by Cambridge fellows through their writings and lectures, which leant weight to beliefs about witchcraft. Most of these dubious works were published by the Cambridge University Press, including Henry Holland's *Treatise against Witchcraft: or a Dialogue wherein the greatest doubts concerning that sin are briefly answered: a Sathanicall operation in the Witchcraft of all times is truly proved: very needful to be known of all men, but chiefly of Masters and Fathers of families &c.* of 1590. Holland was Master of Arts of Magdalene College and, before going to London to be vicar of St Bride's, was vicar of the Cambridgeshire village of Orwell.

Another firm believer in witchcraft was Henry More (1614–1687), a fellow of Christ's College and leader of the Cambridge Platonists. His book *An Antidote to Atheism* was published in 1653. He personally questioned a girl who had been accused of witchcraft in Cambridge and heard from her a lurid tale of a devils' assembly, which he accepted as truth, since it confirmed 'what we heard from four or five witches which we lately examined before'. He similarly accepted as proof of

the reality of witches the most fantastic accounts provided by alleged eyewitnesses including the one concerning 'Old Strangridge of Cambridge who was carried over Shelford steeple on the back of a black Hogge and tore his breeches on the weathercock'. In 1608 the University Press posthumously published William Perkins's discourse upon the *Damned Art of Witchcraft*. Perkins, a fellow of Christ's College and a Puritan, was convinced that witches were in league with the Devil, and that death was the only fitting punishment for them. By publishing this and other books, the University Press added fuel to the fire of persecution that burnt throughout the period, and contributed to the deaths of many innocent men and women.

Fortunately not all academics were so dogmatic, and there always remained a strand of healthy scepticism within Cambridge. One of these sceptics was Samuel Harsnett, Master of Pembroke Hall from 1605 to 1616, and later Archbishop of York. In the 1590s, as chaplain to the Bishop of London, he investigated the case of John Darrell, a Puritan minister, who was charged before the High Commissioners with pretending to cast out evil spirits.

Harsnett's inquiry found Darrell a 'grand imposter and juggler', guilty of 'fraudulent practices'. But Darrell was not without influential supporters in Cambridge who firmly believed in witchcraft. When Darrell published two books defending his actions, copies were sent to William Bradshaw, a fellow of Sidney Sussex College, Cambridge. Bradshaw arranged for a man named Underwood to distribute these popular tracts around the town, much to the annoyance of the vice-chancellor, who informed the Bishop of London. The bishop replied: 'I wolde wish you took souch ordre with the Fellowe that spread them as by lawe you have in that place & keep him in Prison until he shall be content to be examined upon his othe.' Fearing arrest, Bradshaw was assisted by the master of his college, who had purchased one of the books, to escape from Cambridge. Thus, belief and scepticism in witchcraft were evenly matched at all levels within the university and town. The physician William Butler had pronounced Jane Throckmorton to be bewitched but, to their credit, other doctors refused to attribute strange illnesses to supernatural causes.

A prime example is that of the case of a man named Knightley, accused of bewitching two young women in 1604. He was arrested and placed in the custody of the Under Sheriff of Cambridge. No less a person than King James I became involved in the case, writing, via the Privy Council, to the vice-chancellor, Provost of King's College and the Heads of Queen's and Trinity Colleges commanding that they ascertain whether the girls' illness was caused by witchcraft or not. The university arranged for the girls to be examined by 'skilfull Phisitions and learned Devines' but, because 'where there are so many young men diverse out of Novelty may be desirous to see them', the girls were placed in 'the homes of some Townesmen', and no one was to be allowed to see them without authority from the vice-chancellor. The two young women were duly examined by physicians who wrote to the chancellor, the Earl of Salisbury, that: 'very confidentlie and assuredlie they pronounce the disease though somewhat Strange &

extraordinarie & of much difficultie to be cured, yet to be naturall'. The girls were then allowed to return home by order of the king, who also ensured that a sum of £80 was paid to the university to cover their expenses.

Witchcraft mania was at its height in the sixteenth century, but belief in witches has never disappeared completely. In modern times the title has often been acquired by elderly women consulted as fortune-tellers or as advisers on medical matters. At the end of the eighteenth century, a 'wise woman' lived in Falcon Yard, Cambridge, and at the end of the nineteenth century a 'witch', more probably a fortune-teller, lived in Gloucester Street. She was visited one evening by two workmen, one of whom, on the way to the house, said to his companion, 'I wonder what the old b– will have to say to us.' When she opened her door the woman greeted them with the words: 'You'll soon know what the old b– has to say to you, and she'll tell you everything you've said as you were coming here!'

Attitudes towards these 'witches' were not always benign. S.P. Widnall wrote in 1889 that:

> In my young days there lived in one of the pair of old thatched cottages a little way back from the road, halfway from near the village schoolhouse and the main road [at Trumpington], a Fortune Teller, reputed to be a witch, commonly known as 'Mother Sivill'. I believe she was a bad old woman and had to pay periodical compulsory visits to the magistrates and to be punished for her ill-doings. I heard of her sleeping rough in the church porch and also under the trees in the open air. I believe she once stood in the pillory at Cambridge.

BULL-BAITING

BULLS WERE REGULARLY baited at Stourbridge Fair, and particularly on Peas Hill, throughout the seventeenth century, with Hock-tide, the period immediately following Easter, being the most popular time to hold these fights. As with bear-baiting, the bull was chained to a stake either by a hind leg or neck, and sometimes the bull's nose was blown full of pepper to enrage the animal before it was baited (attacked) by vicious bulldogs specially bred and trained for the purpose. The dog would flatten itself to the ground and creep as close to the bull as possible then, darting out, would attempt to bite the bull on the nose or head. The bull, in return, would attempt to impale the dog with its horns and throw it into the air. As with bear-

Peas Hill Market in the early twentieth century; bulls were regularly baited to death here in former times.

A Georgian depiction of bull-baiting: as you can see, the dogs were as much a victim of the practice as the bull, and many of both died during the era of this barbaric sport.

Item, for making bulringe	lljs xjd
Item, for 63 li of lead and a stone to fasten yt in	ixs vjd
Item, for a bushel of stons to pave about yt	iijd
Item, for paving yt	xd

baiting, the university authorities tended to take a dim view of the whole affair:

> ... this plebeian diversion ... when many of the students were too often tempted to join the vulgar throng at the head of whom there were usually assembled a certain description of savages called Bull-haukers who plumed themselves on the merit of producing the best taught bulls for the sport, and dogs also, the most valuable for their courage and dexterity in spinning the poor animal at the stake ... The spinning of a bull is a term applied by amateurs of the sport when a dog has seized his combatant by the nose and holds him tight to the ground with apparent ease.

Despite opposition from the university, the townspeople endorsed the practice for their own enjoyment and, as the Cambridge Town Treasurers' Accounts for the year ending Michaelmas 1604 show, the town paid to erect a bull-ring on Peas Hill:

The university responded by its Statutes of James I of the same year, which forbade bull-baiting within five miles of Cambridge. Despite this regulation, in 1620:

> ... a famous Bull arrived in Cambridge and it was intended that it should be baited at Gogmagog Hills where bowling, running, jumping, shooting and wrestling were to be practiced for a month or six weeks, under the designation of the Olympic Games.

Cambridge student D'Ewes recorded in his diary that, when he and his tutor were returning from a ride past the hills, they saw that booths had been erected in preparation for the fight, and that a little further along the road back to Cambridge they crossed the vice-chancellor 'on his way, as many supposed, to hinder these vain and needless proceedings'.

The town paid for the ring to be set up in 1633, again in defiance of the university statutes:

> 'Item, for settinge up the Bull ringe xvd' and again in 1662 the sum of 9s. 6d. was paid, 'for setting down ye Bull ring on ye pease hill'.

THE ENGLISH CIVIL WAR

CAMBRIDGE'S LOCATION WAS of great strategic importance during the English Civil War (1642–1651), commanding the roads between East Anglia and the Midlands. As a consequence it became the headquarters of the Eastern Counties Association formed by Oliver Cromwell to defend East Anglia. Cromwell, the leader of the Puritan Roundheads, had close links to the town; not only was he elected one of its two Members of Parliament in 1640, but he had also been a student at Sidney Sussex College as a young man, having been born and bred in Cambridgeshire.

Clare College; its building supplies were stolen and used to shore up the castle's defences in this era. (LOC, LC-DIG-ppmsc-08080)

At the outbreak of the war he worked to improve the defences of the town. He first destroyed all the bridges across the Cam, leaving just the Great Bridge, located on Bridge Street. This he defended by strengthening the fortifications of Cambridge Castle, which stands guard above the bridge. To do this he sequestered a supply of building materials that had been acquired by Clare College with the intention of constructing new rooms. This work was undertaken by a garrison of some 300 men, for whom a fort was also constructed within the town.

The long-feared Royalist attack on Cambridge seemed imminent in February 1643, in response to which Cromwell increased the garrison a hundred fold to 30,000 men. His preparations paid dividends, as in the event the king's army thought twice about attacking such a well-defended town and the threat subsided. Cromwell stood down most of the men, but retained an army of 1,000 men in Cambridge for the remainder of the war. Conditions inside the town must have been terrible, with so many men idle for months if not years on end. We know that captured

Royalist officers, and ejected or suspected college fellows, were kept under close surveillance in the Old Court of St John's College, and that King's College chapel served as a drill hall. Supporting such a large garrison demanded vast sums of money, and for this Cromwell turned on the colleges who were obliged to 'donate' money to the parliamentary cause.

The situation worsened in 1644 when the Earl of Manchester arrived to purge the university of men with 'Royalist sympathies'. Only those who subscribed to the 'Solemn League and Covenant', which required zealous endeavour for the 'extirpation of Popery, Prelacy ... Archbishops, Bishops, Deans, Chapters, Archdeacons and all that Hierarchy', were permitted to remain masters or fellows. As a consequence ten masters were ejected and many fellows were dismissed, leading to serious disruption in the teaching of the university. The earl's agent, William Dowsing, ordered the removal and destruction of all church furniture and decoration. Altars, crucifixes, crosses, images and organs were all destroyed in the name of puritanism, and in the process raised money for the parliamentary cause.

Dr Matthew Wren, Master of Peterhouse, and Bishop of Ely from 1638 to 1667, was one of those that suffered during the Civil War. His high church, 'catholic' beliefs and practices had offended the Protestant laity, and in 1642 he was imprisoned in the Tower of London where he remained for eighteen years. During the long years of his imprisonment he vowed that if he

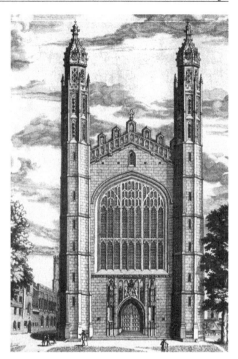

King's College chapel in 1688; during the war, a few decades before, it had served as a drill hall for Roundhead troops. (With the kind permission of the Thomas Fisher Rare Book Library, University of Toronto)

should ever regain his liberty and possessions, he would dedicate his life to the building of a church. True to his word and beliefs, when he was finally released, he invited his nephew, Christopher Wren, to design a new chapel for Pembroke College. The chapel was built between 1663–64 and is Sir Christopher Wren's first complete work, and the first sacred building in England designed in the Classical style. Five years later, and by now a more famous architect, Wren returned to Cambridge where he designed a new chapel with loggias for Emmanuel College.

AD 1658

OLIVER CROMWELL'S MISSING HEAD

YOU WOULD BE forgiven if you had never wondered what had become of Oliver Cromwell after his death, but the story is as intriguing as his life was eventful.

He passed away on 3 September 1658 and, as befitted a statesman of his stature, he lay in state at Somerset House, before being buried with full honours at Westminster Abbey, London, in a ceremony just as lavish as any enjoyed by the monarchy he had fought to destroy. Along with Cromwell lay the other leaders of the parliamentary forces from the Civil War, Henry Ireton

and John Bradshaw. Cromwell's coffin had been buried in the wall of the middle aisle of the Lady Chapel, with the intention that it would rest there for eternity. This was not to be the case. When the monarchy was restored, and Charles II acceded to the throne, as far as the king was concerned, the Puritans were traitors who had committed treason by executing his father, Charles I. In revenge for his father's death, Charles ordered that the bodies of Cromwell, Ireton and Bradshaw be disinterred on 26 January 1661.

Westminster, where Cromwell was briefly interred. (With the kind permission of the Thomas Fisher Rare Book Library, University of Toronto)

On 28 January 1661, the bodies of Cromwell and Ireton were taken to the Red Lion Inn in Holborn, where they were joined the following day by the body of John Bradshaw. All three were then drawn on a sledge to the gibbet at Tyburn; it was the morning of 30 January 1661, the anniversary of the execution of Charles I. The corpses were hanged until sunset 'from morning till four in the afternoon', and then, after eight blows from the axe, Cromwell was beheaded. The disembodied heads were then parboiled and dipped in pitch before being impaled on 20ft-tall spikes at Westminster Hall as a visible reminder to all who passed by of the consequences of regicide. There the head stayed for some twenty years until, following a storm in 1685, it broke free and fell to the ground. A sentry claimed it as a trophy, and despite an official outcry and the offer of a 'substantial reward' for its safe return, on seeing 'the placards which ordered any one possessing it to take it to a certain office ... [he] was afraid to divulge the secret', and so kept it hidden up the chimney of his house.

Down the years the head passed through several hands: in 1710, it was in the possession of Claudius Du Puy, a Swiss-French collector of curiosities, who displayed it in his London museum. It is next found in the possession of Samuel Russell, a colourful character who had once been a comic actor. Russell was possibly a distant relative of Cromwell, and may have bought the head after Du Puy's death to bring it into the ownership of the family. Whilst in his possession the head was seen by James Cox, a wealthy goldsmith and clock-maker, who became besotted by the idea of owning the head, 'convinced

Execution of Cromwell, Bradshaw and Ireton, 1661.

by all the circumstances that it was the identical head of Oliver Cromwell'. Cox offered Russell £100, which equates to about £5,600 today, but 'poor as he was, and considerably in debt, Russell refused to part with it, so dear to him was that which he knew to be the sacred relic of his great ancestor'. Cox was not to be put off, and over the years ensured that Russell gradually became financially indebted to him, so that he eventually had to pass it to Cox in remission of his debts.

It remained with Cox until 1799 when he sold it for £230, the equivalent of £7,500 today, to three brothers named Hughes. Their aim was to establish a museum in Bond Street, and to this end they produced thousands of publicity posters. Unfortunately, the exhibition failed, partly because the entrance fee of 2s 6d, about £7 today, was deemed too expensive, and partly because of rumours that the head was a fake. Despite their failure, one of their daughters continued showing the head to anyone who wanted to see it, whilst efforts continued to profit from the purchase by trying to sell it to a public museum. An offer to sell it was made to Sir Joseph Banks, but 'he desired to be excused from seeing the remains of the "old Villanous Republican", the mention of whose very name made his blood boil with indignation'. William Bullock considered purchasing it, and asked Lord Liverpool his advice. He replied dismissively, that 'the strong objection which would naturally arise to the exhibition of human remains at a Public Museum frequented by Persons of both Sexes and of all ages'.

These failures to sell to public museums forced the daughter to sell it privately. In 1815 Josiah Henry Wilkinson became

its owner. Showing it to Maria Edgeworth in 1822, she wrote that she had seen 'Oliver Cromwell's head – not his picture – not his bust – nothing of stone or marble or plaister of Paris, but his real head'. Thomas Carlyle was less enthusiastic in 1845, writing that although it was 'the head of some decapitated man of distinction ... It has hair, flesh and beard, a written history bearing that it was procured for £100 (I think of bad debt) about 50 years ago ... the whole affair appears to be fraudulent moonshine, an element not pleasant even to glance into, especially in a case like Oliver's.'

The only 'man of distinction' known to have been embalmed, and then decapitated in such a manner over the previous 200 years, was Henry Ireton. Although Carlyle's prominence cast doubt on the authenticity of the head, it has to be noted that Carlyle never actually visited Wilkinson to examine the head for himself. The uncertainty required a scientific answer, and so the head was passed to the eugenicist Karl Pearson, and the anthropologist Geoffrey Morant for a detailed examination. Their 109-page report concluded that there was a 'moral certainty' that the head was that of Oliver Cromwell.

After Wilkinson's death in 1957 his son, Horace, decided that it was time for the head to be reinterred. He contacted Cromwell's old college in Cambridge, Sidney Sussex, and on 25 March 1960 it was buried in a secret location in the college, within the oak box in which the Wilkinson family had kept the head since 1815. The only witnesses to the burial were members of the family and representatives of the college.

AD 1664

PRESSED FOR AN ANSWER: PEINE FORTE ET DURE

PUNISHMENTS IN THE seventeenth century were severe and often brutal. In 1664 a man tried for robbery refused to plead, and as a result 'was sentenced to be and was pressed to death, one hour being taken for the process'. The same punishment was meted out on 9 July 1741 at the Cambridge Assizes when Baron Carter ordered a prisoner, who again refused to plead, to have 'his thumbs twisted with cords'. Finding that this had failed to extract a plea, Carter ordered the man 'be pressed'.

The terrible punishment of the weights: Margaret Clitherow being pressed to death at York.

There was a powerful incentive for suspects to remain mute, as under the law the accused could not be convicted of a crime if they had refused to plead to a charge. They were therefore able to avoid the harsh penalties imposed on those that did. Typically, a prisoner pleading 'guilty' would have their estates confiscated before being put to death, or at best left to face a lengthy gaol sentence. Those pleading 'not guilty' would face a trial of varying degrees of fairness, and if found guilty would again face the loss of both estates and life. Those failing to enter a plea were therefore at a distinct advantage. In order to secure a plea the courts adopted the method of peine fort et dure, legal French for 'hard and forceful punishment', otherwise known as 'pressing'. The accused was laid flat and heavy weights were placed on his chest incrementally until he either pleaded or was crushed to death. It was logical for some defendants charged with capital offences to refuse to plead as by so doing, although they would still die, they would avoid their estates being forfeited to the Crown, allowing their heirs to inherit. The practice was described by the Frenchman Guy Miege, in c.1668:

For such as stand Mute at their Trial, and refuse to answer Guilty, or Not Guilty, Pressing to Death is the proper Punishment. In such a Case the Prisoner is laid in a low dark Room in the Prison, all naked but his Privy Members, his Back upon the bare Ground his Arms and Legs stretched with Cords, and fastned to the several Quarters of the Room. This done, he has a great Weight of Iron and Stone laid upon him. His Diet, till he dies, is of three Morsels of Barley bread without Drink the next Day; and if he lives beyond it, he has nothing daily, but as much foul Water as he can drink three several Time, and that without any Bread: Which grievous Death some resolute Offenders have chosen, to save their Estates to their Children. But, in case of High Treason, the Criminal's Estate is forfeited to the Sovereign, as in all capital Crimes, notwithstanding his being pressed to Death.

Pressing was abolished in 1772, with its last known use having been in 1741. In 1772 refusing to plead was deemed to be equivalent to pleading guilty, but this was changed in 1827 to being deemed a plea of not guilty. Today, standing mute is treated by the courts as equivalent to a plea of not guilty.

ONE IN THE EYE FOR SIR ISAAC NEWTON

SIR ISAAC NEWTON (4 January 1643 [25 December 1642 under the old dating system] – 20 March 1727), a fellow of Trinity College and second Lucasian Professor of Mathematics, is one of the greatest scientists to have ever lived and worked in Cambridge. His credits include the formulation of the laws of motion and universal gravitation, the invention of calculus, the construction of the first practical reflecting telescope and the development of a theory of colour based on the observation that a prism decomposes white light into the colours of the visible spectrum. All this and he still had time to be a Member of Parliament and Master of the Royal Mint.

Just how dedicated he was to his research is demonstrated by his investigation of light, and in particular, 'an experiment to put pressure on the eye'. In Newton's time, little was known about the properties of light; in fact, people weren't even sure whether the eye created light or collected it. Curious, and keen to settle the matter once and for all, Newton embarked on his own detailed study of optics. In order to do this he:

... tooke a bodkine gh & put it betwixt my eye & [the] bone as neare to [the] backside of my eye as I could: & pressing my eye [with the] end of it (soe as to make [the] curvature a, bcdef in my eye) there appeared severall white darke & coloured circles r, s, t, &c. Which circles were plainest when I continued to rub my eye [with the] point of [the] bodkine, but if I held my eye & [the] bodkin still, though I continued to presse my eye [with] it yet [the] circles would grow faint & often disappeare untill I removed [them] by moving my eye or [the] bodkin.

If [the] experiment were done in a light roome so [that] though my eyes were shut some light would get through their lidds There appeared a greate broade blewish darke circle outmost (as ts), & [within] that another light spot srs whose colour was much like [that] in [the] rest of [the] eye as at k. Within [which] spot appeared still another blew spot r espetially if I pressed my eye hard & [with] a small pointed bodkin. & outmost at vt appeared a verge of light.

Newton's interest in performing these experiments was not confined to making optical or anatomical discoveries. He was also concerned to discover whether sensations might actually be the product of the imagination; with what one saw being controlled by the nerves, and thus perhaps by the soul itself.

Newton's notebook describes another experiment to investigate whether the porosity of bodies may have some effect on the colours that they give off, perhaps by hindering the motion of rays of light. To investigate this he experimented with the effects of putting pressure on his own eyeball:

> If I presse my eye on [the] left side (when I looke towards my right hand) as at a, [then] I see a circle of red as at c but [within the] red is blew for [the] capillamenta are more pressed at n & o & round about [the] finger [than] at a towards [the] midst of [the] finger. [That parte] of [the apparition] at q is more languid because [the] capillamenta at o are duller & if [the] finger move towards e two much it vanisheth at q & appeareth semicircular. but if I put my finger at e or s [the] apparition wholly vanisheth. By putting a brasse plate betwixt my eye & [the] bone nigher to [the] midst of [the] tunica retina [than] I could put my finger I [made] a very vivid impression. But of an ellipticall figure because [the] edge of [the] plate [with which] I prest my eye was long & not round like my finger.

Another one of Newton's hazardous experiments involved him looking in succession at the sun, and then at a piece of white paper. He believed that he could replicate what he saw subsequently by imagining that he had looked at the sun 'whence I gather that my fantasy and the

Statue of Isaac Newton, made in 1755 by Louis-François Roubiliac, in the Chapel of Trinity College, Cambridge. (LOC, LC-DIG-pga-02068)

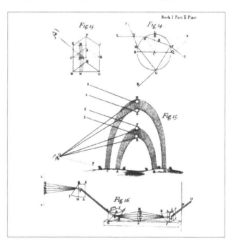

A page from Opticks, showing some of Newton's diagrams of optical phenomena. (LC-USZ62-95334)

Sun had the same operation upon the spirits in my optic nerve'.

Newton's investigations were dangerous, perhaps foolhardy, and certainly painful, but his work laid the foundations for modern science and the technological revolution that it facilitated.

AD 1660–1900

HIGHWAY ROBBERY

HIGHWAY ROBBERY IS as old as the coach route between Cambridge and London. A contemporary traveller complained in his letters that:

> Most intolerable robberies are hereabouts. In 2 or 3 days, 6 or 7 committed – 2 or 3 killed. Last Sabbath within a mile a man knocked on the head. A scholar of Peterhouse both ears cut off, because he told some thieves to whom he had given some money that if they found any more upon him they could inflict what punishment they liked upon him. So finding 20s. by searching they took him at his word and inflicted the cheater's punishment upon him.

This letter brings home the extent of the entrenched lawlessness just beyond the town in 1661, just a few years after the first regular coach service between Cambridge and London had been inaugurated in 1653. Initially the journey took fifteen hours, but improvements to the road after 1663 brought about first by the turnpike trusts, and then by various Acts of Parliament after 1724, shortened the journey time. Despite these improvements, highway robbery proved an attractive option for those finding themselves in dire straits, although the penalty on conviction was final and meant to deter.

A Newgate Calendar illustration showing murderous highwaymen at work. (THP)

One such highwayman was William Osborne who, on 11 April 1829, was executed for the robbery of David Darwood. Darwood had stopped at the Three Horseshoes at Knapwell to break his journey and partake of a meal. He left late in the afternoon in good spirits, feeling refreshed, and was happily travelling along the road towards Conington when a figure stepped into the road ahead and commanded, 'Stand and deliver your money!' Even in the twilight Darwood recognised the figure from his distinctive clothes as a fellow patron of the Three Horseshoes. Darwood stood his ground and shouted back that he had no money, but the reply came back, 'I know you have, and I will have it'. Darwood still refused to comply, and was viciously set upon, being struck on the back of his head by a heavy blunt object, most likely a dibbing iron that Darwood had seen in the possession of the man in the pub. Knocked to the ground and semi-conscious, Darwood was relieved of a considerable sum: twelve gold sovereigns, a bank note and a letter. He was then beaten badly, dragged to the side of the road, and unceremoniously dumped in a dyke and left for dead. The highwayman then made his getaway.

But Darwood was not dead, just badly beaten. After a time he came to his senses and found his way home to Conington. Two days later Darwood was recovering when he saw his assailant, who he recognised immediately; it was William Osborne. The robber was arrested and taken into custody at the castle gaol in Cambridge. He faced trial and was found guilty,

being sentenced to death. Whilst in the condemned cell he admitted the crime, and several others, expressing his regret. On 11 April, following a hearty breakfast, he was taken from the condemned cell to the front of the castle, where in front of a substantial crowd, he was hanged. After the statutory hour his corpse was taken down from the gallows and his body returned to his native village for burial.

If such public executions were meant to act as a deterrent, they failed abjectly, as so-called deterrents usually do; the fact was that people in desperate circumstances will always resort to desperate measures, even when they know the severity of the punishment. Take the case of Cornelius, Francis and William Smith and John and William Taylor, who were brought before the Cambridge Assizes on 26 March 1839 for robbing William Smith on the king's highway.

Smith had been returning alone in the evening from Stourbridge Fair to his farm at Histon when he had been set upon by the five men, who had jumped out of the darkness and held up his horse. A struggle ensued in which Smith lost his seat and became separated from his mount. The robbers pinned him to the ground and stole two sovereigns, along with some silver and his pocket watch. They then stuffed his mouth open to prevent him calling for help, and made their escape. Suspicion fell upon the Smith brothers and their compatriot Taylor, and they were arrested and charged with highway robbery. They came before the court, but the case collapsed when it became clear that the night had been too dark to allow for a definite identification, and they were acquitted. It may have been that, because they were gypsies, and thus outsiders, or perhaps because they were indeed the ones responsible, that 'great suspicion' had fallen on them.

To be robbed on the king's highway didn't necessitate long journeys. William Ratcliff fell victim to a gang at the heart of the town in 1836. He had spent a convivial evening at the Anchor, where he was befriended by Emma Heley, for whom he had bought drinks. The two had then moved on to the Chip Axe pub, where more drink was enjoyed. Emma then invited William to take a walk with her, which he accepted, and the tipsy couple set off down the side of Trinity College towards the river. All of a sudden Emma turned on William and kicked his walking stick from under him, and out of the shadows appeared a gang of men. Their leader was Hugh Fletcher, who knocked William down to the ground, while James Heley, Emma's husband, swore, 'I'll teach you to interfere with my wife!' At which point Fletcher and James Heley were joined by fellow gang members Thomas Pepper and George Benford, all of whom set about William, giving him a severe beating. They also stole the contents of his pockets – just a few shillings – his hat and cane, before the whole party disappeared back into the shadows.

It is not known how long William Ratcliff lay in the street, but he was eventually discovered by a student from Trinity College, who helped him to his feet and took him back to the Anchor pub. As he sat by the fire, coming to his senses, who should walk into the pub but members of the gang of robbers. Bold as brass, one of them was even carrying his stick and wearing his hat; all were still streaked in William's blood. The police were summoned and PC Faiers took the gang into custody. William, meanwhile, was taken into hospital where he remained for eight weeks. On 20 March 1836 the gang, together with Emma Heley, a woman 'of infamous character', came before Justice Gaselee at the Cambridge Assizes. During their trial the thieves exhibited 'hardened and disgusting indifference' to the court, and the proceedings brought against them. Thomas Pepper was acquitted on a technicality, and James Heley walked free through lack of evidence. The remainder, Hugh Fletcher, George Benford and Emma Heley, were all found guilty and sentenced to death by hanging.

AD 1713

BRANDING

FOR **THOMAS TURNER** of Cambridge there was no doubt that 13 really was an unlucky number. On the morning of 29 September 1713, the 30 year old found himself with the Ordinary of Newgate Prison, London, awaiting execution later that day at Tyburn for the theft of a horse. But his luck had first run out in January of the same year when he had been 'burnt in the Hand at Cambridge' for stealing 'sheep and hogs'.

Being 'burnt in the Hand' does not refer to some unfortunate culinary accident but instead alludes to the much more fearful punishment of branding, which had first been adopted by the Anglo-Saxons, but was formalised by the Statute of Vagabonds under King Edward VI in 1547. The branding iron consisted of a long bolt with a wooden handle at one end and a letter of the alphabet at the other; close by would be two iron loops for firmly securing the hands of the prisoner during the operation.

Vagabonds and gypsies were ordered to be branded with a large 'V' on the breast, and brawlers with 'F' for 'fraymaker'; 'T' indicated a thief, 'C' a coin-clipper, 'B' a blasphemer, 'SS' (one 'S' either side of the nose) those who sowed sedition, 'M' a malefactor, and 'FA' a false accuser. The brander would, after examination, turn to the judge, exclaiming 'A fair mark, my lord.' Criminals were formerly ordered to hold up their hands before sentence to show if they had been previously convicted.

An important class of person subject to branding was often granted the benefit of clergy, *Privilegium clericale*. For some lesser crimes, such as petty theft or larceny, first-time offenders were given a more lenient sentence than that normally meted out; in such cases

Administering a brand to a convict. (THP)

the guilty person was branded on the thumb to disqualify them from pleading the benefit of clergy in the future.

In the eighteenth century, cold branding – branding using cold irons – allowed prisoners of higher rank to avoid punishment. In 1782 Charles Moritz, a young German visiting England, recorded in his diary the case of a clergyman who had fought a duel, killing a man in Hyde Park, London. 'Found guilty of manslaughter he was burnt in the hand, if that could be called burning which was done with a cold iron.'

Cases of cold branding led to the punishment falling into disuse, and it was formally abolished in 1829, except for the case of army deserters, who were branded with the letter D, not with hot irons but by tattooing. In 1879 this too was abolished, along with the brand 'BC' for 'Bad Character', applied to notoriously bad soldiers.

BLOODY BURWELL FIRE

THE BLOODIEST CRIME EVER to be committed in Burwell, Cambridge, occurred in 1727 when over seventy innocent men, women and children were burned alive in the village.

The story begins with Robert Shepheard and his players. Robert was a puppeteer on his way to perform with his troupe at Stourbridge Fair, as the Rector, the Revd Borton, recounted in around 1774:

> Some seventeen or eighteen years since a most dreadful accident befell this Town, occasioned by Fire after ye following manner: some stollers passing through here on their way to Cambridge, it being ye time of Sturbridge Fair, had a mind to try their Fortune by acting a Play in this Town in order to raise some Money to put them in a Condition to come to Cambridge.

They arrived at Burwell on 8 September 1727, and Robert probably saw the chance of performing as an opportunity to make a few extra pounds to feed his retinue of players.

It was, after all, something that he and his party did wherever they went. He secured the use of a barn located near to Cockles Row from the owner, Mr Wosson, and set about publicising the performance to the locals of Burwell and the nearby settlements. At only a penny entrance fee, he was happy to fill the barn to capacity. It is hard to say how many people crammed tight into the space, but it must have been at least a hundred; some were even sitting on the rafters. The Revd Borton described the events that unfolded:

> [He] hired a Barn and had a very crowded Audience, as ill-luck would have it, on ye 8th of September, 1727, but before ye Play was half over, and Doors not only locked, but to prevent rude People from forcing themselves in after ye Actors had begun ye Play, nailed by ye Master of the Company for ye greater security.

Just why the door was 'nailed shut', rather than just locked in the normal way is not clear, but it was to prove a fatal mistake as, at about 9 pm:

Fire was call'd out and no possibility of getting out of ye Barn by reason of every Body's crowding to ye Door, which prevented any single Person's being able to force an opening at it; meanwhile ye Barn, which was thatched, and built of wood, and moreover some part of it filled with Straw, was all in Flames, and ye poor unhappy People with-inside either suffocated with ye Smoak or dead with ye Fright and apprehension of their deplorable situation before any Relief could be had from without, so that in a very little space ye Fire was so violent that it burnt ye Barn to ye ground with 72 unhappy wretches.

An ostler, Richard Whitaker, was accused of accidentally starting the fire. That evening he had gone to the barn to feed and water Robert Shepheard's horses, with the intention of staying to see the show. On arrival he had found that he was too late and that the performance had already begun. Believing that as he was there to work he shouldn't have to pay the penny admission charge, he had gone to the rear of the building where a lath and plaster partition separated the stables from the rest of the barn. Entering the stable, he climbed into the hayloft with the intention of working his way toward the partition, through which he would have had a bird's-eye view of the show. Making his way through the loft, carrying his candle and lantern, he accidentally brushed against the hay, which immediately ignited. Within seconds the loft was engulfed in flames, which rapidly spread throughout the

barn. Below, the audience began to panic, and rushed towards the sealed doorway. Nailed tight shut, the door refused to budge, despite the frantic efforts of the audience. Eventually, the door was freed, but it was already too late for some, whilst others were trampled to death in the ensuing crush. In all, over seventy people died. The explanation for quite so many people dying in this tragedy is to be found in the parish register, which records that:

> In the barn were a great many loads of new light straw. The barn was thatched with straw which was very dry, and the inner roof was covered with old dry cobwebs, so that the fire like lightning flew around the barn in an instant. There was but one small door, which was close nailed up, and could not easily be broken down. When it was opened, the passage was so narrow and everybody so impatient to escape that the door was presently blocked up, and most of those that did escape, which was but very few, were forced to crawl over the bodies of those that lay in a heap by the door.

The effort to save people was led by Wicken man Thomas Dobedee, who was first on the scene. He was said to be 'a stout man in the prime of life' who set about pulling people from the fire, and in so doing risked his own life, even to the extent that his hair was singed.

The wind fanned the flames and the fire soon spread to five nearby houses, all of which were burned to the ground. In the process poor Mary Woodbridge, a bed-bound woman, was likewise burned to death. After half an hour the thatched roof of the barn collapsed, and all hope of further survivors was lost. In total seventy-six people perished, and a further two died of their wounds within two days. It is hardly surprising that it was said that every local family had been touched by the disaster.

Richard Whitaker was arrested and charged with causing the fire and the deaths of the innocents. His case came before the Cambridge Assizes in March 1728. At his trial he pleaded innocence, and was able to show that he had been the first person to raise the alarm. As a result he was acquitted of arson, his actions being put down to his negligence rather than to any criminal intent.

That would be that, save for a mysterious report in the *Cambridge Chronicle* which appeared on 19 February 1774, which read:

A Report prevails that an old man died a few days ago at a Village (Fordham) near Newmarket, who just before his death seemed very unhappy, said that he had a Burthen on his Mind which he must disclose, and then confessed that he set Fire to the Barn at Burwell on ye 8th of September, 1727, when no less than eighty persons unhappily lost their lives; that he was an Ostler at that time at or near Cambridge, and that having an Antipathy to the Puppet Show Man was the cause of his committing that diabolical Action which was attended with such dreadful consequences.

The report failed to name the man, but rumour had it that it was none other than Richard Whitaker himself. A tombstone carved with a heart set in an aureole of flames still stands in Burwell churchyard above the grave of the innocent victims.

AD 1738

DICK TURPIN

HAD YOU BEEN able to pop into the Three Tuns Inn on 12 January 1738, you would have found yourself sharing a pint with notorious highwayman Dick Turpin, who had taken temporary refuge in the hostelry. The story of how he came to find himself sat in a Cambridge pub of ill repute is one that has gripped the imagination for centuries.

Richard 'Dick' Turpin (*c.*1705–1739) is certainly the most infamous highwayman of all time. Although he had been involved in criminality from a young age, he began his spree of highway robberies in July 1735. Identified as 'Turpin the butcher', he was first sought for the crime, along with Thomas Rowden 'the pewter', after a robbery on 10 July. Then, just a few

Contemporary sketch of Turpin – here starting at the sight of a gallows – on his way to York. He was to be hanged there in later years. His right leg was seen to tremble as he stepped on to the gallows, where he shortly after threw himself from the ladder, instantly breaking his neck.

days later, the two struck again, this time in Epping Forest where they robbed a man from Southwark, London, of all his belongings. Now with a bounty of £100 on their heads, the two continued to rob on a regular basis throughout the summer and autumn months of 1735. In August they robbed five people on Barnes Common, and shortly after that they attacked another coach party between Putney and Kingston Hill, London. On 20 August the pair relieved a Mr Godfrey of 6 guineas and a pocket book on Hounslow Heath. With the authorities on high alert, the two men were now constantly on the move. First they travelled north to Blackheath in Hertfordshire, then south, back to London, and on 5 December they were seen near Winchester. By late December they had reached a decision that it was safest if they both went their separate ways.

All went well at first, but then Rowden, living under the alias of Daniel Crispe, was caught passing counterfeit coin, and convicted, still under his alias, in July 1736. Eventually his real name came to light and he was transported in June 1738. Turpin's attempts to evade capture were more successful. He made his way to Cambridge, where we find him taking shelter at the Three Tuns Inn on Castle Street. Of all the Cambridge pubs, the Three Tuns was most asso-ciated with felons and ne'er-do-wells, and would have provided an ideal resting point amongst people used to not asking too many questions of rough-looking travellers. It is uncertain how long he stayed in the town, but we next hear of him in March accused of robbing a company of higlers, and then later in the same month working with Matthew King and Stephen Potter. The trio quickly gained in confidence and set about a string of highway robberies. The spree ended suddenly in April 1737. One of the three, possibly King or Turpin, stole a horse from its owner, Joseph Major. Major reported this to Richard Bayes, the landlord of the Green Man pub at Leytonstone, who tracked the horse to stables at the Red Lion pub at Whitechapel, London, where he and Major, along with a constable, sat in wait to capture the thieves. First on the scene was Matthew King's brother, John, who was arrested on entering the stables, and under questioning revealed the location of his brother. The authorities set off to confront the highwaymen and in the resulting firefight Matthew King was shot and fatally wounded:

> ... King immediately drew a Pistol, which he clapp'd to Mr Bayes's Breast; but it luckily flash'd in the Pan; upon which King struggling to get out his other, it had twisted round his pocket and he could not. Turpin, who was waiting not far off on Horseback, hearing a Skirmish came up, when King cried out, Dick, shoot him, or we are taken by G—d; at which Instant Turpin fir'd his Pistol, and it mist Mr. Bayes, and shot King in two Places, who cried out, Dick, you have kill'd me; which Turpin hearing, he rode away as hard as he could. King fell at the Shot, though he liv'd a Week after, and gave Turpin the Character of a Coward ...

According to this account, it was Turpin that fired the fatal shot. Once again Turpin sensibly decided to lay low, moving to Yorkshire later in 1737 where he lived under the name of John Palmer. Once again he took up residence in an inn, but this time local magistrates became suspicious of how he funded his lifestyle. They suspected 'Palmer' of being a horse thief and he was arrested and imprisoned in York Castle. Whilst awaiting trial at the next assizes, he made the mistake of writing to his brother-in-law. The authorities, still on the lookout for Turpin, were keeping his friends and family under surveillance, and intercepted his letter. Palmer was quickly identified as Turpin and on 22 March 1739 he was found guilty on two charges of horse theft and sentenced to death; he was executed on 7 April 1739.

As an interesting postscript, after Turpin's execution in 1739, a glass case containing his hat, cravat, coat, doublet, mask, pistol and spurs appeared at the Three Tuns Inn in Cambridge, where it was displayed for many years with the following notice:

> Be it known to all ye Goodselves That here do come to drink of my Good Beer or to those that do Here Come to Tarry and for to rest their Goodselves and Horses for the night that the clothes Here Set once belonged to Dick Turpin the famous Highway Robber. He on the eve of January 12th 1738 Did'st put up at this Goodly inn as often he did but alack he was sudden surprised by Runners and did have at quick to go just as he was and with only his horse leaving behind his other chattels in my care.

Clearly Turpin was no stranger to Cambridge, as this is the second direct mention of him having spent time at the Three Tuns, and the implication of 'as often did' is clear enough.

AD 1759

COCKFIGHTING

COCKFIGHTING WAS A popular recreational activity, with regular contests held in Cambridge and the surrounding villages. The most important of these took place each Shrove Tuesday on the Market Hill in Cambridge throughout the eighteenth century, and was popular amongst townsfolk and university students alike, although the latter were prohibited from attending the Cambridge fights. Before a fight the cock was fitted with sharp steel or silver spurs designed to fatally wound an opponent in a single strike. Two birds were then placed face-to-face, inches apart, and at a signal from the master of the match the birds were released and the fight began. The contest continued until one bird was killed or badly injured. An even more violent and bloody version of the fight was popular in the eighteenth century – that of 'throwing at cocks'. As the name implies, the aim was to hurl sticks at the birds until they died and, like cockfighting, Shrove Tuesday was an important date in the calendar for this.

Although the university statutes prohibited cockfighting within five miles of Cambridge, this regulation was often ignored. There is even evidence that those responsible for upholding the prohibition often turned a blind eye to it. For example, in 1759 two Cambridge constables were found guilty of failing to report to the Guildhall on Shrove Tuesday as directed by the mayor and vice-chancellor. They had been ordered to attend in order to arrest all those taking part in the throwing at cocks.

Cockfighting was still popular in the nineteenth century, when there was a cockpit in the Green Dragon Inn in Chesterton. Cockfighting was also practiced in public houses in Newmarket Road, as well as in fields on the outskirts of Cambridge. Cocks would be trained for many months, and were looked after by men called 'feeders'. Birds practised sparring every day and were fed and watered after exercise. The correct diet was extremely important, and each feeder followed his own secret feeding programme: brandy, raw steak, maggots and even urine were just some of the varied ingredients used. Charms and spells of biblical or cryptic words were written on small pieces of paper and slotted into the spurs in

The cock pit in Victorian years.

the hope that they would protect the cocks. The last reported cockfight was shortly before the Second World War, when a resident of Cambridge reported receiving an invitation to attend a cockfight at Wicken.

THE RESURRECTION OF TRISTRAM SHANDY

MURMURINGS AMONGST THE students grew louder, distracting Collignon, Professor of Anatomy, from the dissection of the cadaver. Collignon regularly conducted a popular course of twenty-eight anatomy lectures during the Lent term; it was something he clearly enjoyed and seemed by all accounts to fit: a contemporary once described him as 'a most suitable person for the position, as he is a walking skeleton himself'. He stood back from the table and looked at the corpse, and then he saw it for himself. The body lying in front of them was none other than that of Laurence Sterne, the famous author of *The Life and Opinions of Tristram Shandy*. Sterne, who had studied at Jesus College, had died in March 1768, having fallen victim to consumption. He had died in London, where he had been buried in St George's, Bayswater Road, but two days later he had been disinterred by a gang of body-snatchers, known as resurrection men, and sold to Collignon in Cambridge.

Collignon continued with the anatomization of the body, but was ill at ease. Dissection was, and still is, a fundamental part of the study of anatomy, but bodies were hard to come by. Cambridge, in common with London, Edinburgh and the other universities, had resorted to employing the services of resurrection men to obtain suitable candidates for their lessons. This was a shadowy trade, in which discretion was essential, and the last thing that Collignon wanted was to attract attention to his activities. Having a celebrity lying in front of him was a matter of consternation. Thus it was that immediately after concluding his class, the body was hastily removed from the room. The resurrectionists were summoned, and no doubt given a good dressing down for their reckless audacity, before being ordered to return the body to St George's for reburial. They must have followed their instructions, as when the churchyard of St George's was redeveloped in the 1960s, Sterne's skull was disinterred and was identified by the fact that it was the only skull of the five in the shared grave that bore evidence of having been anatomized. It was transferred to its final resting place in Coxwold churchyard, North Yorkshire, in 1969.

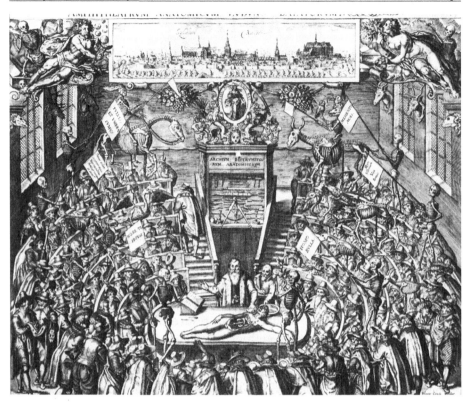

Dissection has been a maligned but necessary feature of medical practice for centuries.
This image, published in 1609, shows an anatomy class about to observe a dissection at Leiden.

Executed felons, suicides and even the victims of drownings, if unclaimed, were all fair game for the anatomy table, but such legitimate supplies fell short of the demand for bodies by the medical school. Even during the eighteenth century, when hundreds of people across the country were executed for trivial crimes, the school had had to resort to disinterred corpses, but the situation became much worse in the nineteenth century, when only about fifty-five people were sentenced to death each year. At the same time the medical school expanded, and as many as 500 cadavers were needed across the country each year. The only alternative was to turn to the resurrection men.

A fifteen-strong gang of resurrectionists exposed in Lambeth, London, in 1795 supplied 'eight surgeons of public repute, and a man who calls himself an Articulator'. As one body-snatcher testified, 'a man may make a good living at it, if he is a sober man, and acts with judgement, and supplies the schools'. The going rate was 2 guineas and a crown for a dead body, 6 shillings for the first foot, and 9 pence per inch 'for all it measures more in length'. These prices were by no means fixed; the black market value of corpses varied considerably. Giving evidence to the 1828 Select Committee on Anatomy, the surgeon Astley Cooper testified that the price for a corpse was about 8 guineas, but also that he had paid anything from 2 to 14 guineas previously; others claimed they had paid up to 20 guineas per corpse. These prices compare favourably with the 5 shillings a week an East End silk weaver could earn, or the single guinea a manservant to a wealthy household was paid. It was no wonder that resurrectionists could 'support themselves and Families very comfortably ... [by] this laudable Profession'. Extraordinarily, at least one London graveyard was owned by an anatomist who, it was reported, 'obtained a famous supply [of cadavers] ... he could charge pretty handsomely for burying a body there, and afterwards get from his pupils from 8 to 12 guineas for taking it up again!'

Prices also varied depending on what type of corpse was for sale. With greater opportunity for the study of musculature, men were preferable over women, and children's bodies were traded as 'big smalls', 'smalls' or foetuses. Anything out of the ordinary was highly prized; the body of the 'Irish Giant', Charles Byrne, brought £500 when it was sold to John Hunter. Parts of corpses, such as a scalp with long hair attached, or good-quality teeth, also fetched good prices, not because they held any intrinsic value to the anatomist, but because they were used to refurbish the living.

Stolen bodies didn't just come from London: in 1753 R. Master wrote that the practice of digging up human bodies in the churchyards of Cambridge and neighbouring villages and carrying them into colleges to be dissected was common. In April 1732 a fresh grave

was found empty in Ditton churchyard, and it was rumoured the body had been taken to Emmanuel College. Obtaining a warrant, a large number of Ditton folk marched on the college, but were refused entry. Enraged, the mob then attacked the walls, provoking students to rise up and defend their ground. Violence erupted between Town and Gown, with punches – and more – thrown by each side. The situation continued to deteriorate to such a point that the Town Clerk was forced to read the Riot Act; then, and only then, would the mob of angry villagers disperse. This, however, was not the end of the matter, as the villagers quite justifiably wanted their loved one returned for Christian burial. They prevailed upon Mr Pern, a Justice of the Peace, for a warrant to enter the college. This was granted and constables subsequently entered the gates to search the college. Needless to say, the woodentops, as they

The bodysnatchers caught red-handed carrying an old woman in a sack. (THP)

were often known, found nothing. Just how cursory the search was is demonstrated by the fact that the following morning the unfortunate corpse was found floating in the pond of the College Close.

Bodysnatching became so prevalent that the relatives and friends of someone who had just died often watched over the body until burial, and then continued the watch over the grave until it had time to decompose, making it worthless to the resurrectionists. Those wealthy enough to afford them invested either in coffins made of iron, or had a framework of iron bars, called a mortsafe, erected to protect the grave. Nonetheless, bodies still went missing, and when they did suspicion fell on the anatomy school. On the evening of 2 December 1833 it was attacked by a mob who mistakenly believed that the body of a pauper was being dissected inside, in contravention of the Anatomy Act. Considerable amounts of damage were done to the building before the mob was repulsed. To prevent similar attacks in the future, it was fitted with heavy iron bars on the windows and doors.

The Murder Act of 1752 required that 'every murderer shall, after execution, either be dissected or hung in chains'. Dissection was generally viewed as 'a fate worse than death' by most people and was intended to act as a deterrent as well as increase the bodies available for dissection. Thomas Weems found himself in this dire situation when, on 6 August 1819, he was executed for the murder of his wife, Mary Ann. At 12 noon he was hanged over the gateway of the county gaol before a vast crowd. After being left to dangle on the noose for the statutory hour, he was cut down. His still-warm body was then conveyed in a cart, under escort from the sheriff's officers and constables, to the Chemical Lecture Room in the Botanical Garden of the university.

Weems was to be put through a particularly grisly and disrespectful ordeal. A powerful galvanic battery was demonstrated by Professor Cumming before an invited and learned audience. He performed a number of experiments, which involved passing an electric current through various parts of Weem's body. When applied to the supraorbital nerve (beneath the eyebrow), and the heel, the most extraordinary grimaces were exhibited: 'Every muscle in his face was simultaneously thrown into fearful action: rage, horror, despair, anguish, and ghastly smiles united their hideous expressions in the murderer's face, surpassing the wildest representations of the Fuseli or a Kean.'

They did not stop there, for the following day his body was opened and placed on view for the public's 'curiosity, disgust and awe'. The doors were then shut, and a large group of learned gentlemen observed Mr Okes perform an extensive dissection of the body. It is no wonder that it was widely held that surgeons were, 'on the whole, disreputable, insensitive to human suffering and prone to victimis[ing] people in the same way that criminals victimised their prey'. Another popular belief was that surgeons were so ignorant of the respect due to their subjects, that they allowed the remains to become offal.

AD 1783

CAMBRIDGE GALLOWS

AFTER JUST FOUR days sat in the condemned cell, George Mean was forcibly taken the few yards to the gallows on Castle Hill, where the hangman placed the noose about his neck and he was unceremoniously hanged. It was 11 March 1783 and Mean had faced the County Assizes earlier in the week where he was convicted of the murder of George Cooper.

The gallows stood in front of the gaol, which up until 1842 was the Norman castle. Originally built to secure the important north–south route that passed through the town, it also played a role in the medieval Anarchy and First and Second Barons' Wars. It was expanded by King Edward I, but then fell into disuse as peace spread across England at the end of the medieval period. With the arrival of the university, the castle walls were dismantled and the stone reused to construct college buildings. During the English Civil War Cromwell garrisoned Cambridge, re-fortifying the castle in the belief that Cambridge would be attacked by Royalist forces. In the event, the predicted battle failed to materialise, and at the end of the war the castle stood empty until the

remaining walls and bastions were taken down in 1785. All that survived was the castle gatehouse, which was adopted as the county gaol. We have a vivid portrait of the gaol at this time courtesy of John Howard, who reported visiting the castle gaoler, Simon Saunders, on 4 February 1782:

> The prison is the gate of the old castle. On the ground floor, called the low-gaol are three strong rooms, one for male felons (30ft by 6ft 7ins); another for women (16ft by 9) with a chimney: the other was not finished. There is an ascent of 22 stone steps on the outside to the debtors' apartments, called the high-gaol. On the first floor is a room for the turnkey, a large kitchen and two or three other rooms. Above them are five rooms and a condemned room. All the rooms are sizeable. Clauses of act against spirituous liquors hung up, by a written order of Thomas Cockram Esq., Sheriff. The act for preserving health of prisoners not hung up. Straw 20s. a year. The castle yard is spacious but not safe and prisoners have not the use of it. In it is the gallows.

1791: A DUEL TO THE DEATH

Until the eighteenth century, duels were mostly fought with swords but, beginning in the late eighteenth century, duels were more commonly fought using pistols, special duelling sets being sold for the purpose. Such was the case when 'a trifling dispute' between Mr Applewhite and Mr Rycroft, both students of Pembroke Hall, resulted in them facing each other on 23 November 1791. The duel was fought near Newmarket, so as to be out of sight of the university authorities. The parties stood back to back with loaded weapons in hand and walked a set number of paces –

Duelling in the late Georgian era.

the graver the insult, the fewer the paces agreed upon – before turning to face each other and shooting. Rycroft was hit and sustained a serious bloody injury.

At first it appeared he had survived this initial shot, but ultimately the wound proved fatal, and he died on 25 November. Under the law, to kill in the course of a duel was murder, but generally the courts were very lax in applying this rule, as they were sympathetic to the culture of honour associated with this 'noble' form of chivalry. It seems that Applewhite escaped not only prosecution, but was not even subject to an official investigation. This attitude towards duelling continued well into the nineteenth century, especially amongst the nobility. When Lord Cardigan was prosecuted for wounding one of his former officers in a duel, Queen Victoria is reported to have expressed a hope that he 'would get off easily'. When he was acquitted on a legal technicality, as she had hoped, there was outrage amongst the middle classes, with *The Times* alleging that there had been deliberate and high level complicity which left a loophole in the prosecution case to allow him to go free, resulting in the newspaper alleging that 'in England there is one law for the rich and another for the poor'.

Although Applewhite walked away from the affair it was not without all consequence. The vice-chancellor of the university found out about the duel and Applewhite was expelled for firing the fatal shot, along with Mr Holland of Trinity College, Rycroft's second. In an attempt to prevent any further repetition of the shooting, the following notice was published by the vice-chancellor:

> Whereas it has been represented to the Vice-Chancellor, that some students in the university have been observed shooting at marks with pistols, an exercise which obviously tends to introduce and promote the dangerous and impious crime of dueling: it is hereby publicly declared, that if any person in statupupillari shall be discovered in the exercise of so unwarranted and dangerous a practice, he will be proceeded against as guilty of a very high offence, and be liable to the severest penalties mentioned in the forty-second statute.

The last English duel occurred in 1845, when James Alexander Seton had an altercation with Henry Hawkey over the affections of his wife, leading to a fatal duel at Southsea.

Debtors have some relief from legacies and donations paid by several colleges: from Sidney College, each has a shirt every year and a sack of coals. From St John's, sixteen penny-worth of bread every Sunday morning. A collection is made in the university and town by leave of the mayor, which amounts to about £7 a year. Twenty shillings, deducting land tax, was also paid from an estate at Croxton.

The gatehouse remained in use as the county gaol until 1842, with public hangings taking place in front of the debtor's door. Large crowds would gather at the conclusion of the assizes to watch the executions, with temporary stands erected around the gaol to allow the maximum number of people to watch, although the best views were obtained from the castle motte, the mound of which can still be visited today. The gaol was run, as prisons were in the nineteenth century, as a quasi-private business. The keeper was paid a small salary of £200 by the county, which equates to about £14,000 today, and expected to make up the rest by charging inmates for basic 'services'. The castle gatehouse was finally demolished in 1842 following the construction of a new

The County Gaol built on Castle Hill. This photograph was taken in 1930, shortly before the gaol was demolished for the building of the current Shire Hall. (H.S. Johnson)

gaol adjacent to it in the grounds of the castle bailey. This new prison was built, following the innovative designs of the penal reformer John Howard, as an octagonal building. Once constructed, prisoners were moved out of the gatehouse, which was demolished to make space for the construction of a new court building.

Nothing remains of either the gatehouse or its replacement gaol, which in turn was demolished in 1932 to allow for the construction of the Shire Hall, which now stands on the site. All that remains of the historic castle is the motte and earthworks, which can be accessed free of charge, giving panoramic views of the city.

THE TRAGICAL DEATH OF THE REVD SAMUEL REEVE

THE INQUEST INTO THE death of Samuel Thressold, aged 18 years, held by the coroner Mr Twiss, found that the late Samuel had prepared a noose before attaching the cord to the rafters of an outbuilding. Then, standing on a conveniently situated beam, he had placed the noose around his neck. Once done, he had tied his hands behind his back before stepping off the beam. Poor Sam was said to have been 'a well-conducted young man' with no symptoms of mental illness and as a result the 'very respectable' jury returned a verdict of *felo de se*. Mr Twiss issued a coroner's warrant for his burial, stipulating that it be between the hours of nine and twelve at night and without the blessing or ceremony of a priest.

Felo de se, Latin for 'felon of himself', is an archaic legal term meaning suicide, as under contemporary common law an adult who committed suicide was a felon, the crime punishable by forfeiture of property to the king. The law was further extended so that anyone who died by whatever cause whilst they were committing a crime was also considered to have died *felo de se*, and thus forfeited

their property to the Crown. Burials for *felo de se* were deliberately made shameful, typically taking place at night, with no mourners or clergy present. Rather than taking place in consecrated ground they were forced out of town, taking place at crossroads or on the borough boundary. Sometimes the poor unfortunate was buried with a stake through their heart. The only exception to this harsh rule was for children and those ruled mentally incompetent, hence the significance of the jury in Samuel Thressold's case considering both his age and mental state. A person considered mentally ill was not responsible for his actions and so could not rightly be punished for his actions. Alas, poor Sam was both too old to be thought a child, and too 'well conducted' to be thought ill.

Driven by the severity of the punishment that a declaration of suicide inflicted on the surviving family of the deceased, there was a move in the seventeenth and eighteenth centuries for juries to find a person *non compos mentis* rather than *felo de se*. Deciding that the person had died as a result of an act of temporary insanity meant that the property was not forfeit to the Crown, allowing the family to inherit. Thus by 1720, over 90 per cent of all suicides were put down to temporary insanity, and in Norwich there was no finding of *felo de se* in the last thirty years of the eighteenth century. This tendency towards leniency in the interpretation of the law can be seen in the case of the death of Samuel Reeve.

The Revd Samuel Reeve MA, fellow of Gonville and Caius and senior proctor of the university, had gone missing sometime after 1 July 1789, the date when he was last seen. His absence was at first noted as unusual, but as time passed his colleagues became increasingly concerned for his welfare. As summer turned to autumn and there was still no news of his whereabouts, the fellows feared the worst. Then on 9 November the college staff, acting under instructions from the fellows, forced open the locked door of a disused storeroom. An earlier search had found nothing to indicate Reeve's whereabouts, but it had been incomplete: they were unable to search the storeroom as the only person known to have a key was Reeve himself. Now that four months had passed without a sighting it was time to resort to more extreme measures, and the door was broken down. One dare not imagine the sight they found, as within the small room, and left hanging by the neck for some eighteen weeks, was the partially decomposed body of Samuel Reeve. At the inquest the coroner's jury still felt justified in returning a verdict of death by virtue of insanity, thus allowing the cleric's burial in consecrated ground and the inheritance of his estate. Reeve

was buried on 11 November opposite the college at St Michael's.

Although it was customary for those who had taken their own lives, and so had died *felo de se*, to be buried in unconsecrated ground, exceptions were sometimes made. On 11 November 1668, Richard Herring, the son of Alderman Herring, drowned himself near the Garret Hostel Bridge. Records show that this was clearly a case of suicide:

> ... he had bin at play at dice the night before being Tewsday night at John Dods at the red Heart in the Petticury and lost (as was thought) there with a London gamester and cheater above 100 which as was thought the onely reason he offered violence to himselfe, the money was said to be taxmoney received by him from Captain Story.

There was no possibility of arguing temporary insanity in this case, and so he should have been buried in unconsecrated ground, but it is recorded that

The Gate of Honour at Caius College (with the Senate House and University Library behind). A fellow's corpse was found locked in a storeroom here.

'He was buryed in the South Churchyard of Gt St Maryes the same night'.

Perhaps his young age and family connections ensured he had the benefit of a Christian burial, albeit one arranged and conducted hastily and with little pomp.

Opposition to the rules governing deaths *felo de se* built gradually, with amendments relaxing them contained in the Burial of Suicide Act 1823 and by the Interments (*felo de se*) Act 1882, before suicide was decriminalised by Section 1 of the Suicide Act 1961.

We know something of the general funeral customs of Cambridge in the seventeenth century from the diaries of Alderman Newton. Wills often provided funds to provide mourners with gloves; it was also customary to provide funds for a mourning ring. Gloves were particularly important elements of funerary etiquette, as his diary entry for the funeral of Alderman John Ewin demonstrates. The funeral was held in All Saints' church, Cambridge, on Sunday, 17 April 1668. Six aldermen carried the body to the church, all wearing gloves and ribbons. Gloves were also worn by the twenty-four common councilmen and the aldermen's wives, but not, he notes, the wives of the councillors. The delicacies consumed on this occasion were '2 sugar cakes and 2 rolls, a cupp of clarett, white and sack'. By comparison, he notes that when Alderman Pedder was buried in St Clement's church on 13 March 1667 only the bearers had gloves, but there were eight escutcheons on the hearse. Heraldic insignia were important at funerals throughout the sixteenth and seventeenth centuries, and clearly impressed Newton.

Newton's diary entry for 15 January 1664/5 describes the funeral of Susanna Wells, wife of Alderman Wells, who kept the infamous Three Tuns Inn on Market Hill in Cambridge:

There was a great funeral [held in Great St Mary's] but little solemnity, many people but small order, the Colledges served in their Colledge Halls, and the rest of the Towne at the 3 Tunns and some other houses neere. She was borne by Mr of Arts, no gloues nor ribbons, seruice one cup of claret, one cup of Ipocras [Hippocras, a cordial drink made of wine flavoured with spices] ... sugar cakes, 2 roles and the best sort onely 2 mackeroons.

Great St Mary's, where the funeral took place.

Funerals tend to be expensive affairs, and those of the seventeenth century were no exception to the rule. The account books of Joesph Mead, fellow of Christ's College, Cambridge, set out in full the funeral expenses of an undergraduate, Ralph Gray, who died only a month after he came up to Christ's College as a fellow commoner in 1618. The eldest son of Sir Ralph Gray of Chillingham, Northumberland, he was buried in the church of St Andrew the Great on 16 July 1618. Mead's accounts also give interesting references to the funeral customs of the day, including the provision of perfume, either to wash the body or scent the room in which he was laid out, and the watching of the corpse by his fellow students:

To the women that laid him out and wound him, being 4, 4s. 0d. For wine & c. to the Schollers that sate up all night with the corse, 5s. For candle and perfumes, 10d. A man that sate up and fetch all things, 1s. Beere, & c. 9d.

His funerals

2 pottel of brewed wine and 16 cakis for the Mr and Fellows meeting in the hall to accompany the herse, 7s. 4d. Borrowing black clothes for pulpit and hearse, 2s. 6d. Pins for verses, 4d. 12 scutchions in mettall, 1li.

Sexton

For making grave, 3s. 4d: Tolling, 4d: Knell, 4d: Sermon bell, 1s: laying the black cloth, 1s: (in all) 6s. Minister, 3s. 4d. His coffin, 6s. 8d. Rosewater, 10d. Breaking a ladder with hanging verses and scutcheons, 6d.

AD 1790s

THE CHIMNEYSWEEP BURGLARS

IT WAS A case fit for Sherlock Holmes and Dr Watson. A college room, securely locked, from within which all the valuables had disappeared. And it happened not once, but several times, to not one, but several different colleges. In each case a considerable haul of valuables had disappeared, apparently into thin air. With no leads to go on, the university offered two rewards, for 100 and 500 guineas respectively – a substantial amount in the 1790s. Following this, the towns-people began to take a pecuniary interest in the university's difficulties and it wasn't long before the good folk of Bell Lane began to suspect one of their own, Richard Kidman.

With little hesitation Kidman was reported to the university, which quickly took action to arrest him. With Kidman in custody, the truth behind the mystery gradually began to unfold. Kidman had two accomplices. The first, William Grimshaw, was a chimneysweep by trade. He had used his craft to map a route through the complex system of college chimneys, which allowed him and his conspirators to enter rooms within which the most valuable items were stored. He had thus been able to evade the most sophisticated of locks by simply climbing down the well-propor-tioned chimneys. Kidman, meanwhile, followed Grimshaw's routes through the chimneys into the storerooms. There he was able to apply his skill as a locksmith, which had enabled him to open the various chests, cupboards and drawers within the chambers, releasing the valuables within. In all this they were assisted by a third man, Henry Cohen, a 'pedlar' and their 'carry man'. His role was to help carry off the booty and then to sell it on.

Grimshaw the sweep was tried first and quickly found guilty; he was sentenced to death. Kidman was next before the court, where he was also found guilty and likewise sentenced to death; however, due to his early co-oper-ation in naming his conspirators, the court agreed to commute his sentence to one of imprisonment. Cohen came next, but the case against him quickly collapsed. With the court unable to make the charges stick, he walked away from the assizes a free man.

ELIZABETH WOODCOCK AND THE CURSE OF THE THREE TUNS INN

WHEREVER WE ENCOUNTER the Three Tuns Inn, we can be sure that trouble is close at hand. February 1799 had been harsh, but despite the intermittent snow, Elizabeth Woodcock set off from Impington and rode into Cambridge for the first Saturday market of the month. Having sold her eggs and butter and made her own purchases, she set off for home at about 6 p.m. Her route took her along Bridge, and then Magdalene Street and up Castle Hill. She should have continued on, but instead was drawn into the Three Tuns, where she stopped for a warming glass of gin: after all, it was a cold winter evening.

After replenishing her flask with brandy, she came out into the dark some time later to find that the snow, which had been falling at intervals all day, was now coming down more heavily. Nonetheless Elizabeth had no choice but to continue home to her husband and children. She rode on and was no more than half a mile from her destination when her horse, Tinker, took fright at something in the night. Rearing up, Tinker dismounted Elizabeth, and bolted off down the bridle path.

Fortunately, she had her wits about her and landed on her feet. Shaken but nothing more, she trudged after Tinker through the thick snow, which was already gathering in the ditches at the side of the road. Finding Tinker a short distance down the path, she was unable to remount, perhaps numbed by the freezing cold, or perhaps as some accounts would have it, because she was too drunk. Instead she took him in hand, and began to lead him back. But the horse was still skittish, and after a short fight, a weakened Elizabeth was unable to control the frightened beast. With one final shake of the neck he broke free of her hold and galloped off into the snowy wilderness.

Tired, cold and not a little worse for drink, Elizabeth found herself all alone, up to her knees in snow, and with a heavy basket of groceries. Home was still almost half a mile away. She struggled on for a few yards, but the situation was hopeless; the last straw came when one of her shoes came off. The only solution, she decided, was to take temporary refuge under the shelter of a hedge growing on the top of a high bank at the side of the road.

There she sat in her heavy snow-sodden clothes while the snow continued to fall, and as it did it began to drift in the steady wind. She must have drifted off to sleep, no doubt encouraged by the contents of her flask, and while she slept the snow continued to pile up around her. She did not know how long she had slept, but when she awoke it was to find that she was now the occupant of an unusual sort of cave formed of the hedge to her back, and a thick wall of compacted snow to the front. The snow was tightly packed about her, so that she could barely move. The hours passed, and then day followed by night, followed by day and yet another night. All the time she sat prisoner, entombed in the cave. She could hear the faint bells of Chesterton church, just a mile away, and sometimes the voices of travellers on the road, just a few yards from her tomb. Finally, on what must have been the following Monday, although weak, she managed with great difficulty to tie her red handkerchief to a short branch from the hedge, which she then pushed through the snow, hoping that it might attract attention. It was not as though people had not noticed her absence. On the Saturday night her horse Tinker had managed to find his way home and, arriving riderless, had immediately prompted a search for Elizabeth. Men from both Impington and Histon had been out in the snow looking for her, shouting out 'Elizabeth Woodcock, where are you? Elizabeth Woodcock, where are you?' Even with her ingenious flag, rescue took time; in fact it was the following Sunday, 10 February, before William Muncey, a young farmer, spotted her handkerchief. The poor man was rather anxious, and slowly approached the spot, peering gingerly through the snow where he glimpsed the eerie sight of a snow-covered Elizabeth. Before raising the alarm he took counsel from a local shepherd and both discussed what to do. 'If it is indeed Mrs Woodcock,' he said, 'it must be part of the dream I had last night, for I dreamed that I should find a hare today.'

The two men walked over to the bank of snow and the shepherd called out, 'Are you there, Elizabeth Woodcock?'

'Yes,' she cried, 'I am here; and it is you, John Stittle, whose voice I hear. For pity's sake, get me out of here.'

Elizabeth had spent eight days buried in the snow, but she had survived. In great pain and suffering from frostbite that caused her toes and fingers to turn gangrenous and finally drop off, she lived until taken ill and died on 24 July aged 43. Hundreds of people came from the country and beyond to pay their respects to the woman who had miraculously survived her long imprisonment in the snow.

Elizabeth Woodcock of Impington, by J. Baldrey.

Impington parish register contains her burial notice:

> On the eleventh day of July 1799 died Elizabeth Woodcock wife of Daniel Woodcock, aged 43 years of a lingering disease in consequence of a confinement under the snow of nearly eight days and nights, that is to say from Saturday the second till Sunday ye tenth day of February 1799.

Below in another hand is written:

> She was in a state of intoxication when she was lost. N.B. her death was accelerated (to say the least) by spirituous liquors afterwards taken – procured by the donations of numerous visitors.

Such was her fame that a small monument commemorating the ordeal was erected near the spot where she was buried. In 1849 it was replaced by another, more imposing one in the presence of 140 people, and a ballad dedicated to her sad tale was sung:

> She was in prison, as you see,
> All in a cave of snow;
> And she could not relieved be
> Though she was frozen so.
> Ah, well-a-day.
>
> For she was all froze in with frost,
> Eight days and nights, poor soul;
> But when they gave her up for lost,
> They found her down a hole.
> Ah, well-a-day.

AD 1846

GENERAL TOM THUMB CAUSES A RIOT

CAMBRIDGE HAS FROM its beginnings as a university town been used to hosting celebrity visitors, but none can quite compare with the visit of the diminutive 'General' Tom Thumb (real name Charles Sherwood Stratton, 4 January 1838 – 15 July 1883) on 10 March 1846. At this time Tom stood just 2ft 5in (74cm) tall and was already one of the most famous men in the world, thanks in part to his showbusiness manager P.T. Barnum, who had taken Tom on his first American tour when he was just 5 years old. This was quickly followed by a European tour carefully constructed by Barnum to make the young Tom Thumb an international celebrity. Thumb, the self-styled 'General', appeared twice before Queen Victoria. He also met the 3-year-old Prince of Wales, who would become King Edward VII. The tour was a huge success, and as his visit to Cambridge neared an end, the university noted how crowds mobbed him wherever he went.

Fearing serious disorder in Cambridge, the vice-chancellor of the university and the heads of thirteen colleges warned students not to take part in any disorderly proceedings. But there was little they could do to swell the enthusiasm and excitement of students and townspeople, and during the course of his visit there were two serious disturbances in the town on 6 March. Following this the Cambridge magistrates swore in a number of special constables to help try to maintain order in the town, but yet more chaos followed over the following two nights. Students and police clashed at a number of locations within the town, including on the Market Hill and close by in Rose Crescent and the Petty Cury. These clashes were violent and at the Lent Assizes, Constable Freestone was found guilty of assaulting a student from Trinity College, Arthur Walsh, and sentenced to fourteen days in prison and dismissed from the force. As the vice-chancellor had feared, the colleges were not immune from the rioting and extensive damage was inflicted on Christ's, Emmanuel, Pembroke and Sidney Sussex colleges, where many windows were broken.

None of this seemed to detract from Tom Thumb's popularity and under the astute management of Barnum, he

King Edward VII (with his son, the future George V, and his grandson, Edward VIII), who as a toddler met 'General' Tom Thumb (inset). (THP)

became a wealthy man. He owned a steam yacht and a house in the fashionable part of New York, where he lived with his equally petite wife Lavinia Warren. Their wedding in New York became front-page news, with some

10,000 guests and a personal blessing from President Lincoln at the White House. Thumb died of a stroke aged only 45 years, and having lived up to his billing as 'General Tom Thumb: the Smallest Person that ever Walked Alone'.

AD 1850

SISTER ACT: THE CAMBRIDGE ARSENIC POISONERS

IN A STORY THAT sounds like it has come straight from an Agatha Christie crime novel, Mary Reeder, aged 20, and Elias Lucas, 25, were sentenced to be hanged for the murder of Susan Lucas. What makes this case intriguing, beyond the fact that their sentence was the last ever public double execution to be performed at Cambridge Castle, is that Mary and Susan, perpetrator and victim, were sisters.

This was a crime of passion, of an affair between Elias and his sister-in-law Mary. The method employed, that most favoured by Agatha Christie, was arsenic. Mary seems most likely to have administered the poison, adding two drams to Susan's meal when the three had sat down to supper together. Susan complained of a bitter taste to her food, then as the arsenic took effect she began to vomit, and shortly retired to bed feeling very ill. She asked that a doctor be called, which her husband dutifully did, but by the time Dr Frederick Crammer arrived, Susan was dead.

If the two thought that their plan was proceeding as they had hoped, they were quickly brought back down to earth. Crammer was suspicious that

Calcraft, who hanged the two Cambridge poisoners. (THP)

a healthy young woman should die so quickly and unaccountably. His examination of the body quickly confirmed that he was right to be suspicious, as she displayed all the outward symptoms of either cholera or poisoning. Given the suddenness of her demise, the latter seemed the more likely of the two. Tests were organised and traces of arsenic were discovered in her body, sealing the fate of her husband and sister.

The two were arrested and taken before the next Cambridge Assizes, where Mr Justice Whiteman tried the case. The pair were found guilty and sentenced to be hanged by the neck until dead. The sentence was carried out on the unlucky couple on 13 April 1850. As was the practice of the time, this execution was a public spectacle. Spectator stands were erected to give a clear view of the gibbet, with the best seats selling for 5s each. The very best views were found by claiming a spot on Castle Hill, and those who arrived early enough to secure their place entertained themselves while waiting for the hanging by pelting the people below with whatever came to hand. By the end of the morning some 40,000 people had gathered to watch the affair. Then, at 12 noon, Lucas and Reeder were brought from the gaol and stood before the debtor's door, where William Calcraft ended the lives of the two murderers. The bodies hung for an hour, as prescribed by law, before being taken down and laid in coffins. The bodies of the lovers were buried together in the prison garden later that afternoon.

AD 1857

THE THREE TUNS INN: DEN OF THIEVES

OF ALL THE public houses in Cambridge, of which there were many, the Three Tuns Inn was the most notorious. It already had a reputation as a resort for thieves and cutthroats in the eighteenth century, when it sheltered notorious highwayman Dick Turpin on several occasions. Although a price was on his head at the time and his identity was well known, no questions were asked of Turpin when he took refuge whilst on the run. After his arrest and hanging, the publican boasted of Turpin's asso-

The Three Tuns in 1936. (E. Rolleston)

ciation with the Three Tuns, and of the trust Turpin had placed in the landlord. To all intents and purposes this was an invitation to those on the wrong side of the law to find sanctuary at the Three Tuns Inn.

It therefore should come as no surprise to find that on 16 January 1857 four men – John Johnson, James Miller, John Smith and ? Williams – all of whom were strangers in Cambridge, were brought before the Borough Court by the authorities. The accusation was made by Jonathan Ambery, an undergraduate at St John's College, who stated that:

> When I came within about 10yds of St Edwards passage I felt and saw an arm put round my throat. I saw no one; my assailants were behind me; I heard the voices of two. I was choked and drawn backwards until I lost my equilibrium.

He complained that he was then 'dashed with violence on to the ground'. His head having been cracked against the pavement, he lost consciousness, during which time the attackers picked his pockets, taking his watch, a papier-

The Three Tuns in 1907. (E.C. Hoppett)

mâché snuff box, a gold pin and about 2*d* in coppers.

This vicious and unprovoked assault was committed on Castle Street, just below one of the windows belonging to the Three Tuns Inn. Hearing the commotion, one of the guests threw the window open and called out. At this a passer-by by the name of Scott was alerted to the incident. Fortunately for Ambery, Scott was an under-porter at Jesus College, and seeing the predicament of the young man, not only came to his aid but was also instrumental in the detention of his attackers. All four were remanded in custody, with John Johnson identified as the garrotter.

BURNED ALIVE

JOHN GREEN WAS the last person to be publicly executed in Cambridge when he was hanged on 2 January 1864. Green was already drunk when he met Elizabeth Green, a 36-year-old woman 'of bad character and intemperate habits' late at night. John took her to the malt house where he worked, probably because his wife and three children were asleep back at the family home. The two drank and talked into the early hours of the morning, warmed by the kiln, and at some point 25-year-old John made an

The interior of the County Gaol in 1930. (H.S. Johnson)

advance towards Elizabeth. She rebuffed him, at which the drunken man became angered and grabbed her by the throat. The two struggled, ending up on the floor, where John's repeated punches rendered her unconscious. Panic-stricken at his actions, and confused by drink, John believed that he had killed the poor woman. Fearing that he would be arrested for murder, he attempted to dispose of her body by burning it in the furnace. He dragged her to the door, but found the body too large to fit inside. In desperation he attempted to crush her limbs, but still she would not fit into the furnace. Next he found some sacks, which he wrapped around the woman, and set about igniting the bundle using red-hot cinders from the fire. The body did catch light and began to burn, but time was running out.

At 5 a.m. William Smedley arrived at the maltings to begin work. He was shocked to discover the still smouldering remains of Elizabeth Green. He could have raised the alarm immediately, but for some reason he did not do so until an hour later. What occurred during that hour will never be known. It is known that William and John were friends, and perhaps John had tried to persuade his friend to help him. Maybe the two had discussed ways to dispose of Elizabeth, only for William to persuade John that the situation was hopeless. Whatever the truth, William did raise the alarm, and for his trouble was arrested and charged with being an accessory to murder and arson. John was of course also arrested, and charged with Elizabeth's murder.

When the result of the post-mortem was released at their trial it was revealed that Elizabeth had actually survived the beating, and had been burned alive by John, death coming by way of asphyxiation from the fire's smoke. Smedley was acquitted at Cambridge Assizes by virtue of having raised the alarm, albeit after an hour's delay, but Green was found guilty. From the condemned cell he would have heard Messrs Bell & Son erect the gallows outside the County Gaol on New Year's Day 1864, and would have known what faced him the following day. Wearing a white smock, corduroy trousers and heavy hobnailed boots he was led to the gallows at two minutes to nine. The hangman removed his hat, but left him with his red handkerchief and placed a white hood over his head. The noose was then tightened around his neck, and the trap door released. Shortly after nine, John Green was dead.

AD 1868

BLOODY STUDENTS: THE BATTLE OF TOWN AND GOWN

IN 1868, RIOTING BROKE out during the parliamentary election in Cambridge. Two undergraduates from St John's College found themselves caught up in the melee whilst going about the town. Looking up, they saw that they were outside the gates of Christ's College and cried to be allowed in. Unfortunately for them the gates were closed and locked tight shut, and the mob of angry townspeople closed around them. Try as they might they were unable to find shelter, as the gates had been firmly barred to prevent the mob surging in and looting the college. The mood of the mob grew increasingly angry, and the cries of the students ever more desperate. Then, and just in the nick of time, as the mood of the crowd had become murderous, a college porter took pity on the young men. Fearing for the lives of the students,

The Battle of Peas Hill, from Gradus ad Cantabrigiam.

he bravely opened the gates to allow the pair to take shelter. His bravery came at high personal cost, for as he ushered them through the open gate a thug from deep within the mob took aim at him with a stone. He was hit on the temple and fell to the ground, where he lay still and quite dead.

Such outbreaks of rioting between Town and Gown have been disappointingly common over the centuries. Fighting between townspeople and members of the university has often proved to be a bloody affair, sometimes lasting two or three days, and leading to severe injuries on both sides, and sometimes even death. Josiah Chater's diaries provide a first-hand account of violence between Town and Gown during the nineteenth century. Living on Market Street, he was often witness to some of the worst violence. For example, his diary entry for 3 March 1846 records that there had been a 'rare row' that evening in the Town Hall and in the streets. These disturbances continued into the following day. Another outbreak of rioting occurred on 7 March, when he records that four undergraduates were arrested. They were charged and on 9 March he wrote:

The four university men were tried this morning at the Town Hall; one was fined £1 10s. 0d.; one 10s. and one 2s. 6d. and pay their costs; the other was let off. There were a very great many people on the Market Hill and the University men vow vengeance to the police tonight. About half past eight the Gownsmen assembled in the Rose Crescent to the amount of, so near as I could guess, 300, and from there they paraded the streets till a little after nine, and then they began to kick up a row – they had tremendous cudgels ... The proctors and Masters were all out, but to no purpose. There has not been such a tremendous row for many years, but after they were all taken in the Gownsmen threw glass bottles on to the Townsmen's heads, and water and stones, which so enraged the Townsmen that they went to all the Colleges and smashed the windows all to pieces – but Christ's has got it worst. There is above 80 panes broken.

Chater, being a townsman himself, is somewhat partisan in his recollections, as the blame always seems to lie with the students. Later in 1846 the famous dwarf 'General' Tom Thumb visited Cambridge. This reignited the animosity between Town and Gown, with the latter making it their business to bar the townspeople from making their way to the Town Hall where the General was performing. Chater is silent as to what the townsmen may have done to provoke such behaviour. Nonetheless, ugly scenes quickly developed as the townspeople asserted their right to go wherever they chose on the king's highway. Reading through Chater's diary for February 1848, we

find him once again complaining of riots between Town and Gown. He records that on the 18th the Gownsmen 'marched about the Town in regiments of about two or three hundred with pokers and all sorts of weapons'. He does not record what weapons the townsmen had, but they must have been substantial as one of the undergraduates had his leg broken and many others were 'very much hurt'.

By the end of the nineteenth century, the level of violence involved in disputes between Town and Gown had much reduced. Misbehaviour amongst students could rarely be described as riotous and is better thought of as (drunken) high spirits. To celebrate Lord Kitchener's visit to Cambridge in 1898 to receive an honorary degree, undergraduates lit bonfires in the Market Place and elsewhere. In order to fuel these fires the students, having exhausted all legitimate supplies of wood, set about the wholesale destruction of wooden shop shutters, palings and just about anything else inflammable that they could lay their hands on. Similar behaviour followed the Relief of Mafeking, and the announcement of the Armistice at the end of the First World War in 1918. Although falling short of the sustained violence of previous decades, such behaviour was nonetheless unwelcome to the residents of the town, and continued to be a cause of animosity toward the university. The fact that records relate how an irate housewife, broom in hand, drove off a mob of undergraduates who were trying to tear up the fence in front of her garden to use as firewood on the occasion of the Relief of Mafeking, shows that this was more youthful misbehaviour rather than serious violence.

AD 1888

FATAL BUMPS

CAMBRIDGE IS AS famous for its rowing races, known as 'Bumps', as it is for its research, and although competition is taken seriously it is not usually thought to be dangerous, let alone fatal, yet history shows just how bloody a sport it has been. A Bumps race is so named because the competing boats chase each other in single file, each crew attempting to catch and bump into the boat in front, without being caught by the boat behind. An annual Bumps race was first held in 1827, but since 1887 races have been held in May and Lent (end of February/ early March) each year.

On 24 February 1888, during one such race, Clare College had bumped the boat from Queen's at First Post Corner. Clare were pulling into the bank when Trinity Hall came into view, hotly pursued by Emmanuel College. Despite rowing at full pelt, Emmanuel caught and bumped Trinity Hall, but such was the momentum of the Trinity Hall boat that it was unable to stop. Instead it crashed into Clare, running over the iron riggers, the pointed prow continuing towards the unfortunate crew. E.S. Campbell took the full brunt

of the impact on the chest, the force impaling him on the prow, which was so great that he was lifted out of his seat. The injured Campbell's chest had been penetrated by the prow cutting between two ribs directly into his heart and, despite frantic efforts on the towpath, nothing could be done to save him, and he died within minutes.

It is not just the participants that risk life and limb by taking part in races; it turns out that it is also a matter of life and death for spectators. On 11 June 1892 an inquest was held at the Pike and Eel pub in Old Chesterton, Cambridge, into the death of Christ's College undergraduate H.C.L. Lovett. Lovett, aged 21, had been struck dead by lightning the previous afternoon whilst walking to the May Bumps. Lovett had been accompanied by a fellow student, Goodman, when there had been a sudden flash of lightning and a crash of thunder. Goodman told the inquest that he had turned round to see his friend 'stretched flat on his back and quite lifeless'. Giving expert testimony, Dr Keene explained that the lightning had struck Lovett at the back of the neck, and gave the cause of death as 'concussion of the spinal marrow'. The jury returned a verdict of natural causes, with death caused by lightning strike.

The Bumps are a highlight of the social calendar, and have always been popular, drawing large numbers of spectators. Nowadays most visitors travel to the races by car, where they park on temporary car parks near the finishing post, and after the races there can be much frustration waiting to get away along the narrow country lanes. At the end of the May Bumps on 10 June 1905, people were also keen to get away. The preferred mode of travel from the finish line back to central Cambridge was by way of ferryboat. Councillor Wallis, who was present at the Plough Inn, reported how at the end of the race there was a sudden rush of people towards the ferry. The *Red Grind*, as it was named,

had been moored at the Plough and was soon full beyond capacity. So many spectators were squeezed on board that Wallis was convinced the flat-bottomed boat would sink, and he and his friends refused to go aboard. Unfortunately he was proved right. The ferry cast off, but had only reached mid-stream when it 'turned turtle' and capsized. About twenty passengers were thrown into the Cam, some of whom immediately found themselves in difficulties. A number of young men bravely dived into the river to rescue them, but for several it was too late. Two ladies, Mrs Thompson of Malta Road and Miss Murkin of Selwyn Terrace, were dragged out already dead; another woman from Bishop Stortford was given mouth-to-mouth assistance and revived, only to die later. The death of Miss Murkin is particularly tragic as she was due to have married the following Monday.

Bumped! A college eight is caught and bumped at the annual Lent races on the River Cam.

AD 1913

SUFFRAGETTE'S PROTEST

A T 1.05 A.M. ON 17 May 1913, a mysterious fire broke out on Storey's Way in Cambridge. Police Constable Smith rushed to the scene, where he found a house ablaze. Then, just as the fire brigade arrived to tackle the blaze, a second fire was discovered in another house. Smith

Women's rights in Cambridge: crowds gather between the Senate House and Great St Mary's during the vote to admit women to titular degrees at the university.

bravely forced his way into this house, noting signs of a previous forced entry that raised his suspicions even further. He found the staircase fully ablaze from top to bottom, and in the next room a strong smell of paraffin and a ladder, wrapped tightly with pink flannelette soaked in the fuel. As he explored further he found yet more rags and paraffin, and then in the kitchen the clear imprints of a woman's feet on the floor. Following the trail back outside he found, under a broken window, first a spot of blood and then a woman's gold watch.

In a time before DNA analysis, it was the watch that provided vital evidence, as it was traced to Miriam Pratt, a young woman of 22 years, who worked as a schoolteacher. Pratt lodged with her aunt and uncle on Turner Road in Norwich, and it was her uncle, a police constable, that recognised the watch as a gift that he had given her some five years previously. He told the investigators that Miriam was an active member of the Suffragette movement, and that she had told him that she was going to the East Cambridgeshire election to deliver leaflets, and had returned home on the evening of Saturday, 17 May.

When confronted by her uncle, she confessed that she had been at Storey's Way and had cut herself as she attempted to get the putty out of the window to remove the pane. She said she was with two other women, one that she named as Miss Markham, while she refused to name the other. Miriam Pratt was insistent she was not the one who had started the fire.

When brought before the Cambridge Assizes, Miriam's uncle gave evidence against her and she was found guilty of arson and sentenced to eighteen months by Mr Justice Bray. Arson was a favourite method of the Suffragettes, often involving setting fire to the contents of pillar boxes in order to garner publicity for their cause. Others demonstrated by chaining themselves to railings, and when imprisoned went on hunger strike. Pratt was not forgotten and whilst serving her sentence the Suffragette press extolled her sacrifice and cause. Then, in October 1913, they saw an opportunity for further publicity when Mr Justice Bray – along with the Corporation and local Magistracy – attended service at Norwich Cathedral. During the Collect, a group of Suffragists rose and chanted the words, 'Lord help and save Miriam Pratt and those being tortured in prison for conscience sake'. Having finished their recital the Suffragists resumed their seats. They were not asked to leave the building and distributed printed accounts of Miss Pratt's defence at the cathedral doors after the service.

THE GREAT WAR

THE USE OF CHEMICAL weapons and high explosives led the First World War to be called 'the chemist's war'. Thus, whilst the outbreak of war led to a mass exodus of students from Cambridge, down from 3,263 students in Michaelmas term 1913 to just 575 by Easter 1916, those that did remain were either medical or science students.

Gas attacks on the Western Front were aimed less at killing soldiers than at disabling them through burns and particularly by blinding them, chlorine and mustard gas being the main causes. Mustard gas was a source of extreme dread as it did not need to be inhaled to be effective – any contact with skin was sufficient. Exposure to 0.1ppm was enough to cause massive blisters. Higher concentrations could burn flesh to the bone. It was particularly effective against the soft skin of the eyes, nose, armpits and groin, since it dissolved in the natural moisture of those areas. Typical exposure would result in swelling of the conjunctiva and eyelids, forcing them closed and rendering the victim temporarily blind. Where it made contact with the skin, moist red patches would immediately appear which, after

twenty-four hours, would have formed into blisters. Other symptoms included a severe headache, elevated pulse and temperature (fever), and pneumonia (from blistering in the lungs).

The Livens Projector was the standard means of delivering gas attacks. Invented by Frederick Livens of Christ's College, it was a simple mortar-like weapon that could throw large drums

Early German protection against gas bombs. (LOC, LC-DIG-ggbain-19551)

Effects of a gas attack. (This photograph may have been posed for training purposes.)
(LOC, LC-USZ62-90494)

filled with toxic chemicals behind enemy lines. Many of those who survived a gas attack were scarred for life. The Medical School focused on training as many medics as it could in support of the war effort, and as a response to the horrific injuries sustained in industrial numbers. A large military hospital was established, first in Nevile's Court in Trinity College, and then on King's and Clare playing fields, now the site of the University Library. A nurse treating mustard gas cases recorded:

Livens Projector, invented by Cambridge man Frederick Livens, in the First World War. (LOC, LC-USW3-004782-D)

> They cannot be bandaged or touched. We cover them with a tent of propped-up sheets. Gas burns must be agonizing because usually the other cases do not complain even with the worst wounds but gas cases are invariably beyond endurance and they cannot help crying out.

The effect was not just to incapacitate the injured, but also to require his fellow soldiers to abandon the fray in order to treat and remove the injured from the battlefield, and of course to induce fear, and thus demoralize the enemy. British

figures from 1916 show that 3 per cent of gas casualties were fatal, 2 per cent were permanently invalid and 70 per cent were fit for duty again within six weeks. To see someone die must have struck fear into all that witnessed it, as death by gas was often slow and painful. According to Denis Winter, a fatal dose of phosgene eventually led to 'shallow breathing and retching, pulse up to 120, an ashen face and the discharge of four pints (2 litres) of yellow liquid from the lungs each hour for the 48 of the drowning spasms'.

In all, of 3,878 members of the university who served in the First World War, 2,470 were killed.

THE JUDASES WHO BETRAYED FROM WITHIN

COVERT MI6 AGENTS in the Baltic, Poland, Albania and southern Soviet Union were all betrayed to the KGB by the actions of Kim Philby. The total number of those murdered as a result of his actions is still shrouded in secrecy and will probably never be known, but it is safe to say that it ran into tens if not

СОВЕТСКИЙ РАЗВЕДЧИК

КИМ ФИЛБИ
1912—1988
5 к ПОЧТА СССР 1990

Russian stamp with a portrait of Kim Philby.
(THP)

hundreds of people, making him indirectly Cambridge's most notorious killer.

To be betrayed once would be bad enough, but to find that he was just one of at least five Cambridge men recruited by the Soviets during the 1930s is still shocking to this day. The Cambridge Five, as they came to be known, met at Trinity College, but Anthony Blunt claimed that they were not recruited as agents until they had graduated. Blunt (codename: Johnson) was a fellow of Trinity College and later MI5 officer, director of the Courtauld Institute, and even Surveyor of the Queen's Pictures. He was several years older than Guy Burgess (codename: Hicks) who became an MI6 officer and secretary to the deputy foreign minister; Donald Duart Maclean (codename: Homer) was Foreign Office secretary, and Philby (codename: Stanley) a senior MI6 officer and journalist based in Washington DC. Blunt acted as a talent-spotter and recruited most of the group except for Burgess. Several people have been suspected of being the 'fifth man', but it is now generally accepted that this dubious honour belongs to John Cairncross (codename: Liszt).

The art critic Brian Sewell, a friend of Anthony Blunt, also implicated a sixth man, Andrew Gow, a Cambridge don who, Sewell suggested, had acted as a 'puppet master' to Blunt.

Central to the construction of the spy ring was the secret society known as the Apostles. Blunt, Burgess, Maclean, Philby and Cairncross were all members of this exclusive, prestigious and – in the 1930s – Marxist society based at Trinity and King's colleges. The members were all well placed in British society and, on leaving Cambridge, went on to successful careers at the heart of the Establishment. As the Queen's adviser on art, Blunt, for example, was knighted in 1956. In 1963, Michael Straight, an American who had also been an Apostle when at Cambridge, admitted to having worked for the KGB, and in so doing named Anthony Blunt as his recruiter. Confronted with Straight's confession, Blunt had to acknowledge his work for the KGB, naming yet another Apostle, Leonard 'Leo' Long as his recruiter. When investigated, Long confessed to delivering classified information to the Soviets between 1940 and 1952. Straight also named the Apostle John Peter Astbury as another spy, having been recruited for the KGB by either Blunt or Burgess.

Burgess and Maclean were about to be uncovered in 1951, but following a tip-off from Philby, they made their escape to Moscow on 25 May, where they were publicly hailed as heroes. Despite their service to the Soviet regime, they were regarded with some suspicion and lived out the remainder of their days, rather unhappily, under constant surveillance. Philby came under suspicion but nothing could be proved and he was officially cleared of any involvement in his two friends' escape. However, suspicion continued within MI6 and, following evidence from a Soviet defector, a fresh investigation into his past was begun. This prompted him to flee to Moscow on 23 January 1963, where he also lived out his days a virtual prisoner.

Although identified as a traitor, Blunt thought that he was safe, having negotiated a deal with the security services which allowed him to keep his title and continue in his role as director of the Courtauld Institute. All this was to change when Margaret Thatcher became prime minister and discovered what had happened. She argued that it was unconscionable for him to be left unpunished and publicly named him as a spy in 1979. Subsequently he was stripped of his knighthood and his honorary fellowship of Trinity College. Blunt withdrew from society and seldom went out after his exposure; turning to drink, he died of a heart attack at his London home in 1983, aged 75. Before his death Blunt conceded that spying for the Soviets had been the biggest mistake of his life, but also went some way to explaining why he had done it:

> What I did not realise is that I was so naïve politically that I was not justified in committing myself to any political action of this kind. The atmosphere in Cambridge was so intense, the enthusiasm for any anti-fascist activity was so great, that I made the biggest mistake of my life.

AD 1939–45

THE ENIGMA OF THE SECOND WORLD WAR

WHEN WAR BROKE out, Cambridge became an important centre for the defence of the vulnerable eastern region of Britain. As well as a Royal Air Force training centre, it also hosted a secret meeting of military leaders in 1944, where the Allied invasion of Europe was planned. But its most important contribution to the war was in the training of

D-Day: Cambridge's breaking of the Enigma code was vital to the success of this mission. (LC-USZ62-111201)

the code-breakers that successfully deciphered the Nazis' secret Enigma codes.

Working at the top-secret Bletchley Park base, a team of Cambridge graduates led by Dilly Knox of King's College, and including the mathematicians John Jeffreys of Downing College, Alan Turing, also of King's and Peter Twinn from Oxford, unravelled the most secret of the German codes during the war. First, in January 1940, was the German Army administrative key that became known as 'The Green'. This initial success led the team of mathematicians to begin work on cracking the 'Red' codes used by the German Army to call in Luftwaffe air support. In cracking these codes not only were countless lives saved, but also the end of the war was hastened.

More than this was the contribution that the team of code-breakers made to the development of the first practical computers. In order to decipher Enigma codes a complex electro-mechanical device, called the Bombe, was designed by Alan Turing and Gordon Welchman, a former student of Trinity and fellow of Sidney Sussex College. The Bombe worked by running through all the possible combinations that the German Enigma machine could generate, leaving a manageable number to be checked by hand. The Bombes were operated by female servicewomen, Wrens, who lived in requisitioned country houses such as Woburn Abbey. The work they did in speeding up the code-breaking process was indispensable.

The greatest of all Bletchley Park's successes was the breaking of the secure communications between Hitler in Berlin and his army commanders in the field. Under Professor Max Newman, St John's College, the 'Newmanry' started to devise machines to mechanise the process of manual deciphering; these ideas were turned into reality by the brilliant General Post Office (GPO) engineer Tommy Flowers. His machine, named 'Colossus', was the world's first semi-programmable electronic computer. Breaking the German codes allowed the Allied staff planning for the invasion of Europe to obtain unprecedented detail of the German defences, saving thousands of lives. The breaking of the German Secret Intelligence Service codes allowed the British to confuse Hitler over where the Allies were to land on D-Day. This led Hitler to divert troops away from the Normandy beaches, which undoubtedly ensured the invasion's success.

FURTHER READING AND BIBLIOGRAPHY

Amongst the various books describing the history and development of Cambridge, I recommend Reeve's, *Cambridge* and Parker's *Town and Gown*, both of which provide authoritative, yet readable, accounts. Porter's *Cambridgeshire Customs and Folklore* remains a favourite read, ideally dipped into for refreshment now and again; whilst Gaskill's retelling of the witch-hunt led by Matthew Hopkins, *Witchfinders*, is an enthralling bedtime accompaniment. Finally, the *Victoria County History* series for Cambridgeshire is the starting point for the serious scholar looking for detailed, if now dated, consideration of the sources.

BOOKS

Armytage, H. 1866. *The Cam and Cambridge Rowing*. Cambridge.

Atkinson, T.D. and Clark, J.W. 1897. *Cambridge Described and Illustrated*. London: MacMillan.

Bateman, J. 1852. *Aquatic Notes or Sketches of the Rise and Progress of Rowing at Cambridge*. Cambridge.

Bevan, W.H. 2010. *Riot at the Garden House*. CAM (University of Cambridge) 61: 22–7.

Bonney, T.G. 1921. *Memories of a Long Life*. Cambridge: Metcalfe.

Bristed, C.A. 1852. *Five Years in an English University*. New York.

Bruce, A. 2005. *Cambridgeshire Murders*. Stroud: The History Press.

Bushell, W.D. 1948. *The Church of St Mary the Great*. Cambridge: Bowes and Bowes.

Bushell, W.D. 1948. *Hobson's Conduit*. Cambridge: Cambridge University Press.

Cambridge University Almanack 1845. Cambridge.

Cantabrigia Illustrata 1688. Cambridge.

Case, T.H. 1885. *Memoirs of a King's College Choirister*. Cambridge: W.P. Spalding.

Cash, A.H. 1986. *Laurence Sterne: The Later Years*. London.

Cockburn, J.S. 1972. *A History of English Assizes, 1558–1714*. Cambridge.

Cooper, C.H. 1842–45 &1908. *Annals of Cambridge*. Cambridge: Cambridge University Press.

Dickens, C. 1885. *Dictionary of Cambridge*. London: MacMillan.

Everett, W. 1866. *On the Cam. Lectures on the University of Cambridge*. London: Ward, Lock and Tyler.

Freemantle, M. 2012. *Gas! Gas! Quick, boys! How Chemistry Changed the First World War*. Stroud: The History Press.

Fuller, T. 1840. *History of the University of Cambridge*. Cambridge.

Gaskill, M. 2005. *Witchfinders: A Seventeenth-Century English Tragedy*. London: John Murray.

Gradus ad Cantabrigiam 1844. Cambridge.

Gunning, H. 1854. *Reminiscences of Cambridge*. London: George Bell.

Hinsley, F.H. and Stripp, Alan, eds. 1992. *Codebreakers: The Inside Story of Bletchley Park*. Oxford: Oxford University Press.

Lethbridge, T.C. 1957. *Gogmagog: The Buried Gods*. London: Routledge and Kegan Paul.

Marsden, J.H. (ed.) 1851. *College Life in the Time of James I as Illustrated by an Unpublished Diary of Sir Symonds D'Ewes, Bart*. London.

Parker, R. 1983. *Town and Gown: The 700 Years' War in Cambridge*. Cambridge: Patrick Stephens.

Peacock, G. 1841. *Observations on the Statutes of the University of Cambridge*. London.

Petty, M. 2003. *Vanishing Cambridgeshire*. Derby: Breedon Books.

Porter, E. 1969. *Cambridge Customs and Folklore*. London: Routledge and Kegan Paul.

Pryme, G. 1870. *Autobiographical Recollections*. Cambridge: Deighton, Bell & Co.

Rait, R.S. 1931. *Life in the Medieval University*. Cambridge: Cambridge University Press.

Reeve, F.A. 1976. *Cambridge*. London: Batsford Ltd.

Roach, J.P.C. 1959. *A History of the County of Cambridge and the Isle of Ely*, Vol. III: The City and University of Cambridge. London: Oxford University Press for the Institute of Historical Research.

Smith, J.J. 1840. *The Cambridge Portfolio*. London: Parker.

Storey, N.R. 2009. *A Grim Almanac of Cambridgeshire*. Stroud: The History Press.

Stubbings, F. 1995. *Bedders, Bulldogs and Bedells: A Cambridge Glossary*. Cambridge: Cambridge University Press.

Varley, F.J. 1935. *Cambridge During the Civil War 1642–1646*. Cambridge.

Venn, J. 1913. *Early Collegiate Life*. Cambridge: Heffer and Sons.

Widnall, S.P. 1892. *A Gossiping Stroll Through the Streets of Cambridge*. Cambridge: the Author.

Winstanley, D.A. 1922. *The University of Cambridge in the Eighteenth Century*. Cambridge: Cambridge University Press.

Winstanley, D.A. 1940. *Early Victorian Cambridge*. Cambridge: Cambridge University Press.

Winstanley, D.A. 1947. *Later Victorian Cambridge*. Cambridge: Cambridge University Press.

Wordsworth, C. 1877. *Scholae Academicae: Some Account of the University in the 18th Century*. Cambridge: Cambridge University Press.

Yeates. G. 1994. *Cambridge College Ghosts*. Norwich: Jarrold Publishing.

JOURNALS

Crook, D. 2006. 'The Cambridge Garden House Hotel Riot of 1970 and its Place in the History of British Student Protests', *Journal of Educational Administration and History*, Vol. 38, Issue 1, April 2006, pp.19-28.

Proceedings of the Cambridge Antiquarian Society.

The Illustrated London News.

Visit our website and discover thousands of other History Press books.

www.thehistorypress.co.uk

Lightning Source UK Ltd.
Milton Keynes UK
UKOW07f0835100115

244289UK00001B/14/P

9 780750 961585